Praise for *Sin Boldly: A Field Guide for Grace*

Here's an utterly original, unflinchingly honest, heart-expanding treatment of my favorite topic: the grace of God. I was so captivated that I missed church while reading it—and Cathleen's lyrical insights refreshed my soul more than any sermon could have. I won't be the same having read it.

—Lee Strobel, author of *The Case for the Real Jesus*

Cathleen Falsani is an excellent writer and a wonderful storyteller. *Sin Boldly* combines these two gifts in inspiring and entertaining stories that remind us that grace is often as unexpected as it is undeserved. This is a book that should be read by anyone who knows they need the grace of God.

—Jim Wallis, president of Sojourners and author of *The Great Awakening*

What makes this book about grace so different and special is that it reads like a novel. It gets the reader to FEEL grace rather than just getting a theological handle on it.

—Tony Campolo, author of *Red Letter Christians*

Throwing caution to the winds, journalist and self-described "freelance Christian" Cathleen Falsani hoists a flag for Grace, impetuously jumping in where angels (and theologians) have feared to tread. Her enthusiasm flies off the page, but there's wisdom, too, as she uses music, art, and story to illustrate her understandings of Grace, that heavenly benison that resists verbal definition but brings faith to vivid life. Her vision of God at work is broad and bold, and I suspect he is smiling!

—Luci Shaw, writer in residence at Regent College and author of *Breath for the Bones*

Sin Boldly is full of hidden treasure and healthy pleasure. Simply put, Cathleen Falsani writes with grace about grace.

—Brian McLaren, activist and author of *Everything Must Change*

Cathleen Falsani reminds us of the immense potential of a life rooted and showered in grace—grace that is ever present in every place if we could just open our eyes and hearts. In fact, the very act of reading *Sin Boldly* is an experience of grace, and you cannot ask that a book be any more wonderful than that. Read this book because it will truly make a difference in your life. But be prepared to laugh and cry and dance, and be ready to live more boldly and love more courageously.

—Rabbi Irwin Kula, president of The National Jewish Center for Learning and Leadership and author of *Yearnings*

In *Sin Boldly*, Cathleen Falsani's frank honesty and firecracker wit guide fellow spiritual seekers along her admittedly crooked Christian journey in search for signs of God's grace. In this faithful field guide, fallen sinners like myself can found hope, knowing that despite our ornery, obstinate, and obnoxious attitudes, grace will crash even our most pathetic pity parties.

—Becky Garrison, religious satirist and author of
Rising from the Ashes: Rethinking Church

Not often do I find a nonfiction book that delights me with Story the way *Sin Boldly* does. With humor, tenderness, and a storyteller's attention to detail, Cathleen Falsani takes us on a ride to show us her world of grace—a grace found in the most unexpected places. Through her honesty and peculiar perspective, Cathleen Falsani made me laugh and cry, and gave me the space in which to believe again.

—Stacy Barton, author of *Surviving Nashville: Short Stories*

CATHLEEN FALSANI

SIN BOLDLY

A FIELD GUIDE *for* GRACE

ZONDERVAN®

ZONDERVAN.com/
AUTHORTRACKER
follow your favorite authors

We want to hear from you. Please send your comments about this book to us in care of zreview@zondervan.com. Thank you.

ZONDERVAN®

Sin Boldly
Copyright © 2008 by Cathleen Falsani

This title is also available as a Zondervan ebook.
Visit www.zondervan.com/ebooks.

This title is also available in a Zondervan audio edition.
Visit www.zondervan.fm.

Requests for information should be addressed to:

Zondervan, *Grand Rapids, Michigan 49530*

Library of Congress Cataloging-in-Publication Data

Falsani, Cathleen, 1970–
    Sin boldly : a field guide for grace / Cathleen Falsani.
       p. cm.
    Includes bibliographical references.
    ISBN 978-0-310-27947-1 (hardcover, jacketed)
    1. Grace (Theology) I. Title.
  BT761.3.F35   2008
  234 – dc22
                                                      2008016853

All Scripture quotations, unless otherwise indicated, are taken from the *Holy Bible, Today's New International Version*™. TNIV®. Copyright © 2001, 2005 by International Bible Society. Used by permission of Zondervan. All rights reserved.

Internet addresses (websites, blogs, etc.) and telephone numbers printed in this book are offered as a resource to you. These are not intended in any way to be or imply an endorsement on the part of Zondervan, nor do we vouch for the content of these sites and numbers for the life of this book.

Published in association with Yates & Yates, www.yates2.com.

Interior design by Beth Shagene

Printed in the United States of America

08 09 10 11 12 13 14 • 23 22 21 20 19 18 17 16 15 14 13 12 11 10 9 8 7 6 5 4 3 2 1

For Anne Moira Sweeney
Full of grace

And in loving memory of Mark Barry Metherell
Good-bye for now, sweet face

Contents

Listen to your life.
See it for the fathomless mystery that it is.
In the boredom and pain of it no less than in the excitement
and gladness:
touch, taste, smell your way to the holy and hidden part of it,
because in the last analysis all moments are key moments,
and life itself is grace.

—Frederick Buechner

Appoggiatura: An Introduction

Why grace?

Because some days, it's the only thing we have in common.

Because it's the one thing I'm certain is real.

Because it's the reason I'm here.

Because it's the oxygen of religious life, or so says a musician friend of mine, who tells me, "Without it, religion will surely suffocate you."

Because so many of us are gasping for air and grasping for God, but fleeing from a kind of religious experience that has little to do with anything sacred or gracious.

Because you can't do grace justice with a textbook, theological definition, but you can get closer by describing it with music and film, pictures and stories.

Trying to explain or define grace is like catching the wind in a cardboard box or describing the color green.

For instance, by way of explaining how Martin Luther defined so-called "common grace," the esteemed Christian Reformed scholar Louis Berkhof, in his book *Systematic Theology*, said such grace "curbs the destructive power of sin, maintains in a measure the moral order of the universe, thus making an orderly life possible, distributes in varying degrees gifts and talents among men, promotes the development of science and art, and showers untold blessings upon the children of men."

That's helpful intellectually, I guess, but for most people it does little toward explaining the experience of grace when we're in its presence. Such a heady definition, while eloquent, isn't something we can exactly wrap our hearts and souls around.

For centuries, theologians have defined, parsed, and categorized grace. Some say there are different kinds of grace. Depending on which flavor of theologian you look to there are two kinds of grace, or maybe three, or seven or nine.

There's common grace and special grace. Divine, irresistible, and prevenient grace. Convicting grace, saving grace, growing grace; protecting, keeping, and dying grace.

Some theologians argue that one kind of grace is better than another, and that some people think they're experiencing "divine" grace when it's actually just "common."

To me, that's like bickering about what color God's eyes are. (They're hazel, in case you were wondering.)

Such arguments remind me of a scene from Woody Allen's movie *Manhattan*, where a group of people is talking about sex at a cocktail party and one woman says that her doctor told her she had been having the wrong kind of orgasm. Woody Allen's character responds by saying, "Did you have the wrong kind? Really? I've never had the wrong kind. Never, ever. My worst one was right on the money."

Grace works the same way. It is what it is and it's always right on the money. You can call it what you like, categorize it, vivisect it, qualify, quantify, or dismiss it, and none of it will make grace anything other than precisely what grace is: audacious, unwarranted, and unlimited.

This is a book primarily for people who say they've never experienced grace, that it doesn't exist, or at least they don't believe it does. It's also for those peculiar folks who relish trying to figure out whether the grace they're experiencing is common or divine. (The answer is, Yes.)

Turning that particular theological lens on my own life, I have attempted herein to describe grace as I have experienced it — in relationship with others, in nature, in my own backyard, and in its most feral state — startling, staggering, and wholly bewildering. In that vein, I embarked on a series of new adventures to see how grace would turn up in travels, in experiences with new people and exotic creatures, in strange lands, and in ways I could not have anticipated had I tried.

This book is meant to point out grace when and where it happens — and I'm an excellent pointer — to show folks what it looks like, tastes like, sounds like. Because everyone experiences grace, even if they don't realize it.

It's kind of like Moby's music. You could ask your average sixty-something-year-old retired banker in Connecticut if he's ever heard of Moby and/or his music and the response you'd receive more than likely would be a resounding, "No—what's a Moby?"

But if you say, "Remember that American Express commercial where Tiger Woods is putting around New York City? Remember the song playing? That was Moby."

"Oh, then, OK. I guess I have heard Moby," our theoretical retired banker in New Canaan might say. "So . . . what exactly is a Moby?"

That's like grace. Not that grace is a pretentious vegan techno-rocker, but you get the idea. Grace is everywhere, all around us, all of the time. We only need the ears to hear it and the eyes to see it.

It is much easier and, I would argue, more helpful to describe what grace *feels* like through stories and images that illustrate the varied ways grace is experienced when encountered in the wild than it is to attempt to define it conclusively, to trap it or cage it.

Maybe that's why Jesus was so fond of parables: Nothing describes the indescribable like a good yarn.

So, let me tell you a story . . .

When I left the newspaper office here in Chicago on the eve of Thanksgiving a couple of years ago, it was sleeting sideways. I had neither gloves nor a handheld windshield scraper thingy, but I did have writer's block, a screaming headache, and a zit between my eyebrows.

Mired in the self-pity ring of my own private *Inferno*, I was feeling anything but thankful.

The worst part of what could have been dismissed as a simple preholiday funk was that I knew exactly how ridiculous I was being for not feeling grateful for the blessings that have come my way — and they are many.

. This unpleasant realization plunged me into the quicksand of self-loathing, which manifested itself most festively in waves of vehicular-induced misanthropy. By the time I arrived home, more or less without incident, about ninety minutes later — a commute that usually takes twenty to thirty minutes — I was so foul of spirit, I had to put my head down for a few minutes and then locate some emergency comfort carbohydrates.

• Hey, no judging.

• If recent news reports are any indication, apparently even God has the occasional need for comfort food. Why else would God and/or the Mother of God appear on grilled cheese sandwiches, fish sticks, and tortilla shells? (Have you noticed that the Divine never seems to turn up in a mixed-green salad or a nice plate of heirloom tomatoes?)

While my take-out lasagna was warming in the oven, I flipped on the TV and found *Bruce Almighty* on one of the 129 HBO channels we get. Sure, I'd seen it before — about a dozen times — but it had just started, and, well, familiarity is comforting, or the devil you know is better than the one you don't, or . . . fine! Jim Carrey makes me laugh. I'm not proud, but it's the truth.

After a few silly scenes, I walked into the other room, leaving Bruce (Carrey) to have his meltdown on the Maid of the Mist at Niagara Falls while I checked on my comfort food.

Not cooking fast enough. Figures, I grumbled to myself, storming around the house, scaring the cats.

Then it happened. The cosmic chiropractic.

I checked my voice mail at work, and there was the message

I'd been waiting for. Good news. Great news, the marvelous, expectation-blowing sort that catches you off guard. By the time I put the receiver down, the pall had lifted. I could see clearly now, the ... um ... sleet had gone.

In fact, the sleet had turned into big, fluffy snowflakes dancing on the other side of my window, decorating the street outside with the first snowfall of the season.

It was beautiful. And the lasagna was ready.

Life is beautiful and I'm an idiot who doesn't deserve any of it.

But that's the thing about grace.

And that's why grace is what I was most thankful for that Thanksgiving. Every Thanksgiving — every moment — for that matter, but sometimes you just see it more clearly than others.

People regularly ask me why I believe in God. The simple answer — and it's MY answer, i.e., it may not be YOUR answer and that's OK — is grace.

As I understand it:

Justice is getting what you deserve.

Mercy is not getting what you deserve.

And grace is getting what you absolutely don't deserve.

Benign goodwill. Unprovoked compassion. The unearnable gift.

Scads of writers and theologians have tried to describe grace, but I think musicians usually get closer to capturing it, sometimes with words, sometimes not. Two of the best attempts I've ever heard are both found in songs. The first is from Bono of U2, in the song he titled "Grace," lest anyone be confused about what he was getting at.

"Grace, she takes the blame, she covers the shame, removes the stain," he sings, in a simple tune that sounds almost like a nursery rhyme. "She travels outside of karma . . . Grace makes beauty out of ugly things."

Yeah, he nails it. That's grace.

But so is what is described in this short lyric from an old Indigo Girls song that may or may not be about spiritual rebirth. It's my favorite idea of grace: "There was a time I asked my father for a dollar," they sing, "and he gave it a $10 raise."

So on the night before Thanksgiving, I moved back to the couch and the TV with my lovely, cheesy lasagna and my spiritual $10 raise to contemplate the recent happy turn of events. The movie was almost over and Bruce was lying in a hospital bed, having just been snatched from the clutches of death by a team of doctors and a pair of defibrillators.

Bruce, who literally had been playing God for a few weeks, looks up at a bag of donated blood being pumped into his veins, and we know what he's thinking. Earlier in the film, he mocked his girlfriend — her name is Grace (played ever-so-graciously by Jennifer Aniston) — for organizing a blood drive.

Bruised, bloodied, and realizing the irony of the situation, Bruce hears a voice and turns to see his long-suffering girlfriend standing in the hospital doorway.

"Graaace!" Bruce says, smiling weakly as tears begin to fill his eyes.

Exactly, I thought with big fat tears running down my own cheeks.

Grace has a way of sneaking up on you like that. When you least deserve it.

That was Bruce's way of seeing and, I suppose, saying grace. This is mine.

Bouncing into Graceland

1

We had moseyed about halfway across the Graceland parking lot on our way from Bubba's pickup to the ticket counter, a few paces past the point where the tail fin of the *Lisa Marie* emblazoned with Elvis's personal logo "TCB" and a thunderbolt appears over the tree line, when a booming voice disrupted our reverie.

"What the heck is TCB?" the man behind us asked no one in particular.

Without turning around to see who had uttered such a question on this hallowed ground, Bubba stopped in his tracks, threw up his arms in disbelief, and bellowed, his own voice dripping with

Mississippi Delta disdain, "Are you *kiddin' me*?! 'Takin' Care of Business in a FLASH!' Come on, man!"

"Actually, I wasn't kidding," said the man, looking more cowed than offended. "I didn't know."

Hhmmph, Bubba grunted and picked up the pace.

I just continued laughing, even though my stomach already was hurting from our fun-filled three-hour drive from Yazoo City, Mississippi, where Bubba's farm is, to Memphis. I didn't have the heart to tell him, of course, that I, too, had no idea what TCB meant before that unfortunate soul asked aloud precisely what I'd been wondering privately.

You have to understand: Elvis is no laughing matter. Bubba and I were on a mission (from God), a pilgrimage nearly twenty years in the making. We'd been threatening to take a road trip to Graceland since we first met as college freshmen in Chicago in the late 1980s. We finally had made it to Elvis's home, and a certain amount of decorum and respect was due as we approached the visitor's center.

"Gloooooory, glory Haaaaaahleeeluuuuuuuuuujah," Bubba sang, doing an impressive (and loud) impression of the King singing the "Battle Hymn of the Republic" portion of his signature "American Trilogy" while we waited in line to purchase our "Elvis Entourage VIP Tour" tickets. For $68 apiece we received laminated VIP passes on lanyards, didn't have to wait in line with most of the other tourists, and got our pictures taken in front of a blue-screen Graceland backdrop. (We had them made into nifty refrigerator magnets!) It was all terribly exciting and long overdue.

Bubba is my "best good friend," as in Forrest and Bubba in *Forrest Gump*. He calls me Kitty and I call him Bubba, even though neither is close to our given names. We can't remember why we adopted those particular nicknames—inside jokes lost to our approaching-middle-age memories. Nevertheless, they stuck. Since we were both eighteen years old, we've gone together like peas and carrots. (I'm the carrots.) It is an entirely unlikely friendship, miraculous you might even say. Bubba is a politically conservative Presbyterian, cotton-farming, goat-herding good ol' boy from Mississippi. And I am ... really not. We bonded quickly over the one thing we did have in common, a mutual obsession with music—to this day I can't hear Elvis or Steve Earle without thinking of him and, often, picking up the phone to tell him so.

I don't remember how we first met, but we both recall vividly our first marathon conversation in the lobby of Fischer Dorm at Wheaton College. We talked about relationships, more specifically about our unrequited crushes on, respectively, the gorgeous bad-boy son of a preacher and a tall, willowy blonde teen model with the sparkling wit of a kneesock. Neither would give us the time of day, much to our utter soul-crushing dismay. Bubba determined that my beloved was a truckload of trouble that I was better off avoiding. I insisted that he had a problem with liking the women who were completely wrong for him. In hindsight, we were both spot-on. After that long night (we talked until dawn, if memory serves), we would spend hours driving around in the powder-blue Saab he had christened the "Pork Chop Express," listening to music and talking about life. I accompanied him to buy his first 12-string guitar, and he came with me to see my first Springsteen concert. On the way home from that particular show, my Tahitian-green-pearl Honda Civic ran out of gas on a deserted stretch of highway south of Chicago. Bubba is the only human being I know who could get me to laugh about being caught in that kind of predicament, even when we were in the back of a police cruiser on the way to a gas station with a cop who was decidedly not a fan of the Boss.

Bubba is my proof text for disproving the *When Harry Met Sally* assertion that men and women can't just be friends without at some point becoming romantically involved. He is closer to me than a brother, but we've never had anything other than familial love for one another. Our extraordinary friendship is one of the great blessings of my life, clearly a gift from God because the intervention of the Holy Spirit is the only way to explain our improbable, time-tested bond. When we were freshmen, I read a book in my Theology 101 class by the British theologian John V. Taylor called *The Go-Between God*. In it, Taylor argues that the presence of God can be experienced as much *between* people as in them, and that God's grace is what makes the connections between people that wouldn't happen otherwise. That's how I got Bubba. It is the only legitimate explanation for how this liberal journalist, freelance Christian, Connecticut Yankee and the self-proclaimed "high-tech hillbilly" pride of Yazoo City, Mississippi, formed a lifelong bond. For the grace of our friendship, I am ever grateful.

When I called Bubba a while back and suggested we finally make that pilgrimage to Graceland — stunningly, neither of us had been there on our own in the intervening years — he thought it was a great idea. When I told him I figured the trip to Graceland would be great research for a book about grace, he was skeptical. "I know some people think Elvis is God, but what in the world does Graceland have to do with grace?" he said.

"Trust me, Bubba," I answered. "You'll see."

Still, when I arrived at his house in Yazoo City, Bubba cornered me in the kitchen and, good five-point Calvinist that he is, proceeded to lecture me on his thorough and erudite theological understanding of grace, and his concern that many Christians might misunderstand it as a kind of "get outta jail free card" to sin, if not boldly, at least with abandon. "Thank you, Bubbs, but this trip isn't a pop quiz on the theology of grace. It's about the experience of grace," I explained. He still looked skeptical.

Later, in his inimitably funny way, Bubba admitted he might be overthinking the whole concept of grace. "Us five-pointers should be the ones to understand and convey grace the best, but we're not," he said. "But grace has got me in a headlock and won't let me go."

Yep. Precisely.

What Bubba didn't get at first is that he is grace to me. His friendship is one of its most vivid manifestations in my life. It is a gift, unearned and totally unexpected, one that neither of us ever could have orchestrated on our own. And this grace has appeared most powerfully not in the having each other as a friend but in *being* friends, knowing that we would step in front of a train to save the other, that there isn't anything one of us could do to make the other throw up our arms, storm away, and slam the door forever. We show each other grace, we are grace for one another, and I'd like to think we inspire each other to be gracious to the rest of the world.

Bubba makes me laugh harder than anyone I know. One of my favorite definitions of laughter comes from the modern Christian rebel/apologist Anne Lamott, who describes it as "carbonated holiness." I like to think of laughter as grace in its gaseous form. It's the kind of grace that can lift you out of a funk and lighten a heavy spirit. It's sort of like that scene in *Mary Poppins* where Bert and Uncle Albert are laughing so hard that they start to levitate, literally floating to the ceiling. Sometimes all it takes to turn a dark mood on its ear is to hear Bubba's goofy drawl on the other end of the phone saying, "Hiya, Toots! What's shakin'?"

We were uncharacteristically solemn during our tour of the Graceland mansion on that hot July afternoon. There's a lot about Elvis that is easy to mock, and believe me, we have. (We cracked ourselves up to the point of tears when we toured the *Lisa Marie*, Elvis's Convair 880 jet, and Bubba spotted the custom-made queen-size bed with a blue suede coverlet and FAA-regulation giant seat belt and threatened to hop over the security rail and duck under the covers while I took a picture.) But there's also something tragic and endearing about Elvis's life story. I should mention that when Bubba and I first met, I wasn't a big fan of the King. But Bubba took great pains to explain, at length and occasionally with scriptural support, the brilliance of Elvis's music, performance, and persona. Eventually I came around, and we've shared a rabid love for the King, even going so far as to send greeting cards to one another on January 8 (Elvis's birthday) ever since.

Did you know the only Grammy awards Elvis won were for gospel recordings? It was one of the many surprising bits of trivia I took away from our pilgrimage to Graceland, the famously kitschy Memphis home where Elvis lived — and on August 16, 1977, died. The King of Rock 'n' Roll won his first Grammy in 1967 for Best Sacred Performance for the recording of the gospel album *How Great Thou Art*. His second Grammy, for Best Inspirational Performance, came in 1972 for his gospel album *He Touched Me*, and a third in 1974 for the recording of the song "How Great Thou Art." Offstage, Elvis, who was reared in an Assemblies of God church in Tupelo, Mississippi, spent hours singing gospel tunes with his entourage as a way to relax and, perhaps, self-soothe.

According to what his daughter, Lisa Marie Presley, says in the audio tour Bubba and I listened to as we spent a couple of hours moving reverentially from room to room in Graceland, Elvis was a real spiritual seeker, especially later in his troubled life. He was always looking for something and read loads of books on religion and spirituality.

One of the most interesting and poignant displays at Graceland is Elvis's desk. With a built-in radio and TV, it was a state-of-the-art gift from his label, RCA Victor. On it were several spiritually themed books, including a copy of Khalil Gibran's *The Prophet* and Erich von Däniken's *Gods from Outer Space*. I guess he still hadn't found what he was looking for. Or had he? A book I read shortly after our trip to Graceland argued that Elvis was raised as and remained a genuine Christian believer all of his days. As a kind of proof, the author, one of Elvis's former backup singers, revealed that at the time of his death, the record on the turntable in his bedroom — perhaps the last music he ever heard — was a recording of his favorite gospel songs. Many people — many Christians, for that matter — might scoff at the idea that Elvis, with all of his overindulgences, addictions, and peccadilloes, also could have been a believer. I think Bubba and I both left Graceland with the bittersweet impression of Elvis as an incredibly gifted, tragically flawed man who lavished love and outrageous gifts on his family and friends, desperately tried to reconcile staggering fame with personal heartache, but in the end felt alone, empty, and lost.

Yet the faith that Elvis had as a child, and that Bubba and I share, promises that it doesn't matter whether he could pull it together in the end. Grace fills that gap. While it's true that you may lose your religion during the course of a lifetime, you never lose your salvation. Once you let Jesus in your kitchen, he just keeps on making peanut butter and banana sandwiches, and he never leaves.

Such an illustration of grace reminds me of something I experienced at Bubba's farm the day after we returned to Mississippi from our little pilgrimage. We were out in the pasture with some of the two hundred purebred and percentage Kiko goats he began raising a few years back. One young billy goat kept getting its head stuck in the fence and wailing until Bubba patiently would walk over and gently lift it out of the wire tangle. We were there with the goats for about fifteen minutes, and that dopey goat got its head stuck three times. Each time, without yelling or even displaying his frustration, Bubba calmly helped the goat out of the trap and put it back with the rest of the herd. I think that's what Jesus, the good shepherd, does with those of us who try to follow him but keep screwing up.

When we start squealing for help — every time, without fail — he comes to the rescue, frees us from the prison of our own making, and lovingly puts us back in the flock with the rest of the goats.

*Above all the grace and the gifts
that Christ gives to his beloved
is that of overcoming self.*

—Saint Francis of Assisi

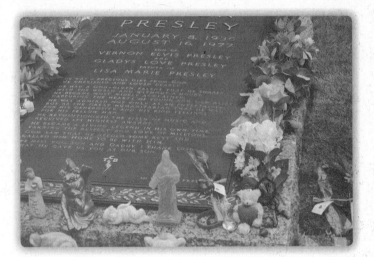

Walking in Circles 2

Maybe it was the pebble in my Mary Janes.

Or maybe it was the distinctive fragrance of cornflowers in the hot sun. Verdant. Earthy. Familiar, like the way my mother smells — of Chanel No. 9 and translucent dusting powder — before she goes out for the evening with my father.

Whatever the catalyst was, one late summer afternoon while I walked the labyrinth at St. Scholastica Convent on the far north side of Chicago, I was transported to my grandmother's yard in New Hampshire about thirty years earlier.

It was a beautiful August day. I was a wee girl. And I was happy, but I had a pebble in my Mary Janes. Back then, I recall stopping in my tracks and whinging until someone helped me remove the tiny offending rock.

But now . . . no.

I walked a long while with the pebble in my grown-up Mary Janes. It didn't hurt. It was just a nuisance, like so many things in life can be, distracting us from the beauty of the moment. In fact, after a few minutes, as I shuffled alone through the labyrinth's dusty, rocky path, I began to enjoy the pebble as if it were a pause button in the time-space continuum.

As the labyrinth's path doubled back on itself once, twice, and again, I forgot about the pebble and noticed things I hadn't on the first pass. Delicate lily pads in a small reflecting pool. A Japanese lantern tucked inconspicuously next to a short hedge. A red-winged blackbird watching me from a low tree branch.

Have you ever walked a labyrinth? Literally, I mean. I hadn't until that summer afternoon at St. Scholastica. I'd often meant to, and I'm fairly sure I've seen a few over the years (the lovely one in the footprint of St. James Episcopal Cathedral in downtown Chicago comes to mind), but I'd hadn't taken the time—or the spiritual space, actually—to walk one.

A labyrinth is an ancient symbol—a spiral formed by a circuitous yet single path that leads to a center and back out again—dating, some historians say, to at least 2000 BC. The ancient Greeks, the Celts, and the ancient Egyptians, among many other early cultures, incorporated the labyrinth into their mythologies.

Prehistoric labyrinths were considered, variously, traps for evil spirits and patterns for ritual dances. In the medieval era, the labyrinth acquired a new ecclesial meaning—the symbol of a difficult path to God where the entrance is the same as the exit.

The labyrinth at St. Scholastica follows a historic pattern perhaps best exemplified in the labyrinth elaborately inlaid on the floor of the nave of Chartres Cathedral in France. The Rogers Park version is far less sophisticated. And that is its charm.

Hidden behind a large garden of vegetables and flowers accessed through the monastery's service entrance off the busy Ridge Avenue, red bricks outline the labyrinth's forty-foot-wide pattern. Its paths are filled with pebbly sand.

A vined trellis in full bloom beckons walkers on one side. A few simple stones—one a rough-hewn rock inscribed with the name of a nun—mark the entrance and exit, which are one and the same. There are benches and swayback wooden chairs here and there along the perimeter and on the lawn surrounding the labyrinth.

There are no directions.

That's because there's no wrong way to walk a labyrinth.

I should explain what brought me to St. Scholastica in the first place. A few days before my visit to the labyrinth, I had watched a short film sent to me by the kind folks at Spiritual Cinema Circle (www.thespiritualcinemacircle.com) who distribute groovy short films, documentaries, and spiritually themed feature films that otherwise might never be seen by a wide audience.

The short film, written and directed by and starring the (apparently) exceptionally industrious Scott Cervine, is called *Closer Than Ever*. In it, Scott, playing a character named Colin, has run out of room for his spiritual life among the distracting effluvia of modern living.

He used to practice yoga with his sweetheart. They used to

meditate. He used to have time to think, to be quiet, to just . . . be. But these days Colin is in overdrive—that is, until he has an encounter with a couple of cheekily meditative monks at a monastery.

When an orange-robed monastic meditating blissfully on a cushion with his eyes closed motions for Colin to join him, he declines.

"You're afraid," the monk says.

"Excuse me? I'm afraid? I'm the one who's afraid? Mr. sit-by-the-fountain-and-do-nothing-all-day—and I'm the one who's afraid?" Colin asks, incredulous.

"He just means running away is a symptom of fear," a second monk tells Colin. "If you stay, you might find . . . what you're looking for."

When the first monk insults Colin—he calls him a "big, fat, noisy mama's boy" who's afraid to stay and face the unknown on his own—Colin takes it as a triple-dog-dare.

"Look, crazy monk people, I don't know what's going on here. Apparently, there's some lesson," Colin snaps, sarcastically. "I got it. You wan' a lesson? Let's go, baby," he says and, after cracking his knuckles and stretching, plops down on a blanket next to the monk and begins to meditate.

The distractions come, as they always do. He checks his watch, falls asleep, and swallows a bug, all the while watching the monk out of the corner of his eye.

Colin is trying to compete. But meditation is not a competitive sport. Neither is faith. There isn't one singular, correct way to practice it. In the end, you have to walk the path to God or away from God on your own.

I am an ENFP. You know, on the Myers-Briggs personality test. Extroverted, intuitive, feeling, perceiving — and fiercely competitive. I want to make sure I'm doing it right — whatever *it* is — all the time. And most of the time I want to make sure I'm doing it better than you are.

At the gym. In the yoga studio. At the office. In church.

Oh yes, my friend. In church.

As a teenager in Sunday morning service or at a youth group hymn sing, I strove to make sure I was singing the contralto harmonies just right with a perfect vibrato making curlicues at the end of my notes. If it was a praise song, I wanted to make sure my lifted hands (in praise to God, of course) were waving as gracefully and expressively as possible, like a holy hula dancer. And I'd want to be sure my prayers were beautiful, heartfelt, and perfect.

But as my tenure in (spiritual and physical) adulthood wears on, I've discovered — thank God — that all of that is thoroughly wrongheaded and simply impossible.

There is no right way. There is no best. There is no perfect. It's not a competition. Not when it comes to faith. Not when we're talking about our relationship with the divine. In the end, it's about grace; it's about something you don't do. It just is.

One unusually mild January afternoon recently, I took a power walk in the village where I live, traveling a route that takes me past the childhood home of Ernest Hemingway and about a dozen Frank Lloyd Wright houses and Lloyd Wright knockoffs we call "Bob Lloyd Wrights." I follow the same basic course almost every time I walk, but this day I started one street farther east than usual, and that's when I saw it — a labyrinth in the lawn next to one of the dozens of churches in our village, a house of worship I had driven by many times but don't often pass on foot. I don't know how long the labyrinth has been there, but I'd never noticed it before that day.

I was just gearing up to the "power" portion of my walk, gaining speed and picking an up-tempo song on my iPod (something from the frenetic Scottish band The Fratellis), when I spotted the labyrinth. Instead of letting it wait for another more languid trip, I stopped my workout, found a mellower soundtrack (Coldplay) and entered the labyrinth. I was about two-thirds of the way through the pebbly warren when I noticed a burst of motion out of the corner of my eye. I turned to see three young children—a boy and two girls about five or six years old—bolting toward the entrance of the labyrinth. Huge smiles spread across their faces as one said, "Ready? GO!" and they took off, racing each other along the labyrinth's narrow path toward the center. One of the girls grew impatient and cut across lanes to the center before giggling and skipping away toward the church. I continued to walk at my slow, adult-contemplative pace until I reached the center, where I stopped and watched the kids run along the path toward me. The two remaining children—a brother and sister—continued to race at full throttle, kicking up gravel as they skidded into turns. The boy reached the center first as his sister stopped in her tracks, gave up, and strode off looking dejected. "Good boy, Jack!" the kids' mother called from a few yards away.

More of the time than I'd like to admit, I'm Jack, racing toward the middle, trying to be the fastest, the best, and determined to beat out my sisters and brothers along the way. Rather than walking the labyrinth at my own pace, I'm constantly comparing myself to others and picking up speed, headed toward the goal that I think is ahead, quite sure of precisely what the goal is, and hoping that someone will yell "Good girl, Cath!" when I'm the first one across the finish line.

But that's not how it works, is it? All you can do is walk the path, wherever it takes you, into the future or into your past.

Remember, it's not a maze. There are no dead ends. The way is always clear, if we open our eyes to see it.

It's not a race, so stop to smell the flowers along the way, bask in the warmth of the sun, enjoy the silence, allow the peace to embrace you. And rest a while at the center before making your way back out into the world.

One day I walk in flowers
One day I walk on stones
One day I walk in hours
One day I will be home

—Bruce Cockburn

Driving and Crying 3

   After being in the newsroom around the clock for a couple
of days after the terrorist attacks of September 11, 2001, I came
home exhausted and broken—spiritually, emotionally, mentally.
I collapsed on the futon and turned on the TV just as U2 began to
play live from London during the international 9/11 telethon.

> *And if the darkness is to keep us apart*
> *And if the daylight feels like it's a long way off*
> *And if your glass heart should crack*
> *And for a second you turn back*
> *Oh no, be strong*
> *Walk on, walk on*

It was precisely what I needed to hear. Not from a rock band, not from any other human being. It's what I needed to hear the Creator of the Universe say.

That moment of grace in the guise of a song reminds me of something I once heard the author Frederick Buechner say: "Pay attention to the things that bring a tear to your eye or a lump in your throat because they are signs that the holy is drawing near."

One perfect summer night a few years ago, the holy, as it does, snuck up on me in the most random of places. A peachy gloaming lit the western skyline as I drove home, top down on my ancient Miata, through the quiet rough-and-tumble streets of Chicago's west side. Blaring from the tinny speakers I'd cranked up to almost 11 was one of those songs that makes me sing at the top of my voice (even in a convertible) and throw my hands in the air — "You Can't Always Get What You Want," by the Rolling Stones.

Driving while listening to music is one of life's great pleasures. It's a spiritual practice I learned from my father. When I was a little girl and he was working on his doctorate at Columbia University in New York City, sometimes I would accompany Daddy on the ride from our home in Connecticut into Manhattan. Many of my fondest memories from early childhood are of those regular road trips in his Karmann Ghia, whizzing along the Henry Hudson Parkway, listening to his favorite traditional jazz station on the AM-only radio, talking about nothing in particular, and eating Cracker Jacks from the box he always kept in a hidden compartment behind the cushions of the backseat.

Years later, when I got my driver's license, I would spend hours driving back roads, singing along to cassette tapes of my favorite bands or the alternative radio station out of Long Island that I could tune into in the car but not in my bedroom at home. I do my best thinking in the car, taking the scenic route and the long way home to stretch even a quick run to the supermarket into a contemplative journey, alone with my thoughts and some righteous tunes. There's something about the insulated solitude of a car that gives me permission to sing with abandon while working on various existential conundrums.

As I rolled up to a stoplight near the United Center (home of the Chicago Bulls and Blackhawks) that summer night, the Stones song ended and a familiar voice took to the airways, hitting me upside the head with some unexpected spiritual wisdom, leaving me gobsmacked (or, more accurately, God-smacked). It was Lin Brehmer, the radio station's most popular disc jockey, reading one of his "Lin's Bin" essays, this one an answer to some listener mail—a letter from a fellow in Indiana who asked, "I'm not getting any younger. Should I start going to church? If so, which one?"

The DJ's answer, in part, was this:

> As we get older, we begin to consider our mortality. The godless man might ask himself at the end of his life, "Have I miscalculated? Should I have communed with my maker?" Even W.C. Fields, a man known more for his hatred of kids than his love of religion, was discovered late in life with a Bible on his hospital bed. "Bill," a friend, asked, "what are you doing reading the Bible?" and Fields replied, "Looking for loopholes." . . . Finding your faith later in life brings a different perspective to religion. Still, watching a child you know grow up and solemnify their belief in front of family and friends will move you in mysterious ways. Is this the same baby in a stroller now chanting in Hebrew? A sweet three-year-old girl I know was once at Mass, and as the bewildering experience wore on, she became impatient

and began to squirm. Her mother tried to placate her by pointing out a picture of the Christ child. In a voice that reverberated to every chamber of the stone cathedral, the innocent shouted, "I HATE THE BABY JESUS!"

Now, here comes the part that got to me, taking me by surprise and bringing tears to my eyes. "Before you wonder at the consequences," Lin said, "remember what Jesus himself said: 'Suffer the little children, and forbid them not to come unto me,' because *I can take it.*"

Whoa. That's about as profound a religious statement as I've ever heard. And it's not exactly what you might expect to hear between rock anthems on Chicago's premiere rock 'n' roll radio station. But WXRT is not your average radio station and Lin Brehmer is not your average disc jockey. He is known, in fact, as "The Reverend of Rock 'n' Roll." It's a moniker Lin earned in the early 1970s when he was a young DJ in Albany, New York, where he hosted a show on Sunday mornings. It's a nickname fellow jocks bestowed on him because of his proclivity for reading from "Book Nine" of John Milton's *Paradise Lost*, particularly the line that says, "Shall that be shut to Man, which to the Beast is open?"

"OK, mister, I think it's time you and I had a chat about this 'Godstuff,'" I told "the Rev." in an email after I heard him read the essay titled "Choosing Faith," the one that had moved me so deeply. Never one to flee from a dare, Lin gamely acquiesced to a thorough grilling in his office at the radio station, and, as is often the case when I go looking for God in the places some people would say God isn't supposed to be, what I discovered was much more intriguing than I could have imagined.

I have a favorite T-shirt that reads, "Jesus is my mixtape." When I bought it, I thought its slogan was charmingly quirky, but over time it has acquired this transcendent quality, a motto that sums up my belief that everything—everything—is spiritual. At the center of that everythingness, as a pastor friend of mine likes to describe it, is a universal rhythm, a song we all play, like a giant, motley orchestra. Sometimes in tune, sometimes off-key. We call it by different names. Still, it remains—if only we have ears to hear it—the eternal soundtrack that plays in the background of our lives.

For the nearly twenty years that I've called Chicago home, WXRT has provided the (literal) soundtrack to my life. It was the first radio station I tuned to when I arrived in Illinois in the fall of 1988 to start my freshman year at Wheaton College, and it's still the station I'm tuned to while driving or cooking in the kitchen or just puttering around the house. Since 1991, except for the days when I oversleep, Lin has been the morning mixtape master, spinning the music that starts my day. In 2002, Lin began reading on the air his thrice-weekly "Lin's Bin" essays, running the gamut from the silly ("The Hokey Pokey: Is That What It's All About?" for instance) to the blatantly spiritual.

The morning I turned up at the radio station to grill Lin about God, he had just finished his morning broadcast and was reaching for an ancient, bedraggled copy of *Norton's Anthology of English Literature* (in two pieces with no cover) as I walked through the door of his office. "I've always been fascinated by religion and man's relation to the divine," Lin told me flipping pages in the book to find *Paradise Lost* so he could read from his favorite passage. "I'm a mystical expressionist," he says. "I take the idea of mysticism very seriously, but I sort of paint it my own way. I think the idea that there is something within each and every one of us that can take us to a place we've never been before is what makes it great to be alive."

Music is a vehicle that propels Lin—and me and so many other people—toward a place we might call Grace. Music is part of our cultural conversation, and in nervous times like these, it has a lot to say. The idea that music has the power to move people in a way nothing else does seems never to be far from Lin's mind. "People ask me why I got into radio," he says, "and for me, it was almost always a musical thing, almost as if I wanted to preach by playing songs that said something."

The musicians that shaped his consciousness as a teenager— Jimi Hendrix, Jim Morrison, the Beatles—were more than just drug-addled rock stars. They were prophets, Lin says, warning us about the future, just like Jeremiah and Ezekiel did in the Hebrew Scriptures.

Modern musical prophecy didn't end when the Summer of Love drew to a close in 1968. Lin keeps on his desk at the radio station a framed picture of his teenage son, Wilson, playing a blue Fender Stratocaster guitar. It reminds him that music has the same effect on Wilson and his peers that it did on his father as a teenager. "I absolutely think that teenagers or young people are as much affected emotionally and spiritually by the music they hear as by any sermon they hear in a church," he told me without a hint of bitterness or sarcasm in his voice. "Part of the reason I have trouble going to church and staying in church is feeling like the sermon some minister is espousing wasn't connecting with me in any way, whereas a good four lines from a John Hiatt song could mean so much more to me."

As someone who had her first spiritual epiphany at the age of twelve while listening to U2's "Gloria" for the first time after school in a friend's living room, I can attest to this. The message can even be the same—sometimes, as was the case with "Gloria," the words themselves are the same—as what we hear in church or temple, mosque or shul. But there's something mightily powerful about hearing the words sung aloud with passion or pathos, as a guitar wails and a bass line thumps.

What brings a tear to the eye of one person is not the same thing that puts a lump in the throat of another, but for everyone there is some music that changes their life. Whether it's some pop cutie-pie on *American Idol* warbling a song written by committee or Tom Waits grunting through "Swordfishtrombones," there is some music that gets inside of everyone. For Lin, it's music such as "Good Day for the Blues" by Storyville, "Gimme Shelter" by the Rolling Stones, or Bob Dylan's "It's Alright, Ma (I'm Only Bleeding)." For me, it might be Jeff Buckley's "Hallelujah," "Not While I'm Around" from the Stephen Sondheim musical *Sweeney Todd*, or "Nessun Dorma" from Puccini's opera *Turandot*. (The rousing, climactic verse, *"Tramontate, stelle! All'alba vincerò! Vincerò! Vincerò!"* reduces me to a puddle every time I hear it.)

"You talk about what your religious faith is supposed to do for you and what a minister or a rabbi is supposed to do for you, providing you with counsel and wisdom and sustenance and support—sometimes the quickest avenue to all of those things is a song that you love," Lin says. This reminds him of music he also associates with 9/11. "The day after September 11, I opened my show with a song I never play just as a *song*. Now it's the first song I play on the anniversary of 9/11 every year. It's called 'Sunflower

River Blues' by John Fahey. It's a very simple acoustic guitar instrumental. But for me," he says, leaning forward in his chair, his voice dropping, "it has that same feel as the second movement of Beethoven's Seventh Symphony."

"Dunnnn dun dun dun, dunnn dunn, dunn dun dah dunn—it kind of plods along, but there's a kind of resolution in the musical phrasing, and it's the same thing in that John Fahey song. It's got a certain melancholy feel to it, but at the end it kind of resolves itself in a major chord that makes you think everything's gonna be OK," he said, smiling wistfully. "It's gonna be all right."

That day at the radio station, as Lin expounded on music's more mystical qualities, I became aware of a song playing quietly on the radio receiver on his desk tuned to WXRT. It was U2's "Walk On." When I mentioned it to Lin, he turned up the volume, and we were both struck still, as if an unexpected third party had just joined us.

I know only enough of God
to want to worship him,
by any means ready to hand.

—Annie Dillard

Via della Conciliazione   4

Rounding a bend in the dark cobblestone streets of Borgo Santo Spirito just before 1:00 a.m., the bodies heaped under blankets that lined the sidewalks and doorways evoked images of Calcutta rather than Rome. I could hear people talking in hushed tones but couldn't pick up the conversations until one man's voice rose above the murmuring din.

"For an industrialized country, this is primitive," the Italian gentleman sniffed in English as he passed a particularly rowdy collection of humans huddled together against the cold in front of some church steps on the narrow old street behind St. Peter's Basilica.

"Primitive, yeah!" a young American's voice with a distinctly Chicago flat twang responded. It was Angie, a student at Loyola University in Rome, one of a group of young people I'd met the day before and planned to join as they camped out overnight in order to get a spot as close to the basilica as possible for Pope John Paul II's funeral the next day. I had been searching for them, and Angie's joyful voice was like a beacon guiding me to them.

"Hey, wanna sit down?" Angie asked when she spotted me approaching the group. "We can squish. Squish over! Squish over! Ever played Phase 10? It's really fun! We can teach you how to play. Want some water? How 'bout a sandwich?"

The Italian poet Cesare Pavese once said that we don't remember days; we remember moments. Of the frenetic month I spent in Rome in April 2005 covering the death of John Paul II and the election of his successor, Benedict XVI, I am hard-pressed to remember individual days — what I did when, which story I wrote on which day, or even what event came before or after another. But my memory is rich with sensory snapshots that play in my mind like a slide show — vivid glimpses of grace:

On the overnight flight to Rome, watching Chicago's Cardinal Francis George calmly reading the Italian newspaper *Il Messaggero* while the jetliner hit some rough turbulence and how he didn't flinch, how his paper even didn't flutter when the plane dipped violently and the rest of the passengers gripped the armrests — and thinking, *There is a man comfortable with his mortality.*

Walking the jam-packed streets of Vatican City among some four million pilgrims from around the globe who had come to pay their respects to the late Pope John Paul II in the days leading up to his funeral, peacefully standing in lines a mile and a half long and thirty people deep for hours just to spend a few seconds in front of his body as he lay in state inside St. Peter's — and hearing them sing or pray the Rosary in Italian, Polish, English, French, German, and languages I couldn't decipher.

Strolling behind St. Peter's one evening, the tawny light from a narrow doorway catching my eye as it shimmered off the damp cobblestone street — and looking inside and seeing several dozen faithful prayerfully climbing a staircase on their knees.

Nibbling a cone of hazelnut gelato on a warm spring afternoon in St. Peter's Square when smoke appeared from the chimney atop the Sistine Chapel and feeling the crush of humanity behind me as thousands poured into the square to see whether it was white or black; sensing electric anticipation when the smoke was gray and then a few minutes later when it became clear that the smoke was white and that a new pope had been elected; the rumble in my chest as a massive cheer went up in unison; watching the *campanone* (a huge bell under the clock on the left side of the basilica that's rung when a new pope has been chosen) swing forward before I could even hear the sound of its first toll.

On my first free day after working nonstop for more than a week, taking the first sip of a perfect bellini made with fresh peach nectar at an outdoor café and watching tourists wander from church to church in the Piazza del Popolo, and savoring the sweet smell of the rosewood rosary beads I bought from a street vendor as I turned them in my hands.

The most unforgettable memories I have from that trip to Rome are of the night I spent sleeping (or, rather, not sleeping) on the streets of Vatican City with the Loyola University students. Angie's effusive hospitality and generosity were typical of the grace-filled phenomena I'd watched overtake the city in the days leading up to the ritual when the world would lay Pope John Paul II to rest. The crowds that night were extreme, but so very kind. Determined, long-suffering and faithful. "Papa," as many of the college kids I met referred to the late pontiff, would have been pleased.

For the next few hours, bundled together on a patchwork of blankets and sleeping bags, the kids attempted to teach me how to play the card game Phase 10. After a dozen or so hands of the game I never quite caught on to, we sunk into easy conversation about the historic events we'd all witnessed in the past week. We talked about the mundane effluvia of life for a while, and then they turned their attention back to more eternal things.

The Loyola students were joined by a number of seminarians from The Pontifical North American College, a graduate-level seminary where many American men come to study for the priesthood. In the wee hours of the morning, after games and idle conversation had petered out, one of the seminarians, a gentle-spoken third-year seminarian from Montana named Mark, suggested the group pray together. For the disposition of Papa's soul. For the safety of the millions of people who had crowded into Rome for the funeral. And for divine favor—they asked for God to help them get a plum spot from which to watch the funeral. It was a very sweet prayer, almost childlike.

A little more than an hour later, after individual entreaties were lifted to God and the group had prayed several decades of the Rosary while successfully facing off with a street-cleaning machine that had tried to unseat them from their spot on the Borgo, and after a couple of the seminarians had disappeared to kibitz with a kindly Italian police officer guarding the gates to the Via della Conciliazione (the wide boulevard that leads directly into St. Peter's Square), our little group of pilgrims found itself being let through the barricades and onto the Via several hours ahead of hundreds of thousands of others.

"That's the way God is; he really blesses," Mark said as we rushed to scout a prime location on the Via—not too close to the square but not too far either, and within eyeshot of two jumbo TV screens, just in case. "We just walked up and down, just praying, saying, 'Lord, if it's your will, let this group get in.'"

Once we chose a spot on the boulevard, the group settled into the peaceful predawn hours—some sleeping, some praying quietly. It gave me time to reflect on whom I was with and what we were about to experience. How appropriate that I should be with college kids for the pope's homegoing, I thought. Giovanni Paulo, as the Italians called him, had a special affinity for young people. In the weeks and months before his death, hundreds of teenagers, known as "Papaboys" for their devotion to the ailing pontiff, stood vigil in the square outside his residence. Supposedly John Paul II's final words were addressed not to the loyal friends and assistants at his bedside but to the crowds of young people chanting up at the window to his papal apartment overlooking St. Peter's Square.

He said, in Italian, "I looked for you; now you have come to me, and for this I thank you."

Perhaps the most striking thing about the crowds that had descended on Rome to pay their respects to the late pope, apart from their sheer mass, was the number of young people in their midst. They were everywhere, in every nook and cranny, alcove and Internet café, gelateria and church pew, in this city-state, singing and praying and flirting and sleeping and waiting and waiting and waiting for their chance to say good-bye. Their presence at what had become a kind of Woodstock for the pious flew in the face of popular wisdom that said kids today are missing a moral center, that their spirituality was vague at best, that they were too caught up in the things of the world to give two hoots about anything transcendent.

A few days before the pope's funeral, I asked Cardinal George what he made of all the kids in the crowd, many of them not Catholic and some of them not even Christian. He said the most extraordinary thing about what he believed drew them to this place at this moment in history: "Holiness is always contemporary. Some people wonder why an old man — feeble, barely able to walk, barely able to talk in the last weeks — is so attractive to young people. It's because of his integrity, certainly, and young people respect that. But it's also because of his holiness. It's sin that makes us old. Holiness is always young. And the pope died a young man."

Sometimes the holy draws nigh to us. And sometimes we are drawn to the holy.

About 5:00 a.m., in the predawn chill, I was tired and cranky and feeling every one of my thirty-some years. I wondered whether camping out was the best approach to covering the funeral story. Perhaps it would have been better — easier and more efficient — to have taken a more traditional, civilized approach and shown up in the media holding area close to the platform where the funeral would take place at a reasonable hour, fresh with sleep and wearing comfortable shoes.

My self-doubt session was interrupted by the arrival of several small white vans that pulled simultaneously onto the Via della Conciliazione a few yards from our makeshift campground. Wide shutters opened on the side of the van, and a handful of people dressed in the uniform of the Italian civil service beckoned to the few groups of pilgrims asleep on the street. Slowly, people began to wander toward the van, and I could see steam rising from its open window. Those inside were distributing warm croissants and hot sweet tea to whomever needed refreshment.

I can still taste that tea. Warm. Tender, if a beverage can be tender. Rejuvenating.

As we sat there with our cups of tea and hot pastries, the sun began to rise over the boulevard. One of the seminarians took out his guitar and began to play a familiar tune. We sang "Our God is an awesome God" while the sun crept higher in the sky, chasing away the night's chill.

When the police opened the main security gates at 6:00 a.m. and tens of thousands of eager pilgrims carrying flags from their homelands ran down the Via della Conciliazione toward the basilica, Angie and I clung to a large potted palm tree like cowboys in a stampede. We watched the emotional three-hour funeral Mass perched on the rim of the tree's huge planter, standing among its rough, prickly branches, with a world-class view.

It's funny. I don't remember much of the funeral Mass itself. I can recall the faces of people in the crowd who were mourning, surely, but who shared a look of bliss that smoothed the edges of their grief. Basking in the face of the holy is how I would describe it. The specifics of who said what during the pope's funeral are lost in my memory.

But the events of that long night before—the grace of being huddled together and praying with strangers, the surprise of being let through to the street early, the sense of anticipation and long-suffering, and the taste of that tea as sweet and life-giving as the sweet Holy Spirit itself—I cannot forget.

Drink your tea slowly and reverently,
as if it is the axis on which the whole earth revolves—
slowly, evenly, without rushing toward the future.

—Thich Nhat Hanh

Watermelon Gazpacho

5

The car stereo gave out just as the rains began. Hour thirteen of a fifteen-hour drive from Chicago to the Mississippi Gulf Coast.

I was singing along with Springsteen's song "The Fuse" when the radio went dead.

> *Blood moon risin' in a sky of black dust*
> *Tell me Baby who do you trust?*

Fussing with the tuner and giving the speakers a couple of quick slams, I looked back up at the road just in time to see graffiti on the highway overpass in big blue letters that answered, "TRUST JESUS."

Cute, Lord, I thought. *Now what?*

Silence.

The rain persisted in a maudlin drizzle, just hard enough for me to switch the wipers on their lowest intermittent setting, and the skies grew grayer and moodier as I pushed on down the road toward Bay St. Louis.

Alone with my thoughts and the rhythmic swishing on the windshield, my mood grew darker, too, as I turned the car onto Route 90 heading east. That last fifteen-mile stretch of the trip could not have been more depressing, as I motored past the corpses of broken trees and moribund buildings interrupted by the neon scream of an occasional fast-food joint. The geography felt sad, as if it's always raining there, a perpetual storm that hadn't stopped since murderous Hurricane Katrina roared ashore nearly two years before, all but leveling the storied beach community known as "the Bay."

Always wet. Puddles forever. A persistent damp.

I checked into the one sad-sack motel I had been able to reserve online, and it did nothing for my case of the bobies — a vague sense of disillusion and doom based on nothing in particular. Just kind of *meh.* I recall the interior of the motel room being an anemic shade of mint green, with a healthy case of mildew adorning the walls like spotty black wainscoting. The room was clean, but it felt dank and the carpet was clammy. It was late afternoon when I arrived in Bay St. Louis, and I was starting to feel peckish. From the drive down Route 90, I figured I'd be dining on Taco Bell, and as enticing as that prospect was, I decided to delay my run for the border for a half-hour or so and take a drive toward the waterfront.

At 10:00 a.m. on August 29, 2005, Hurricane Katrina made

landfall at high tide in Bay St. Louis with 135-mile-per-hour winds followed by a thirty-foot storm surge that obliterated pretty much everything in its wake. Upwards of 90 percent of all structures in the Bay — a picturesque artist's haven with historic inns, galleries, renowned restaurants, and bohemian boutiques — were destroyed. Aerial photographs of the town's waterfront taken after Katrina hit show the first two blocks of the downtown business district simply washed away. Nearly two years after the worst natural disaster in United States history befell this small community about an hour's drive east of New Orleans, the rebuilding had begun, but there were still many people living in FEMA trailers. And as I drove from the motel toward the beach, for every structure in the process of being mended or rebuilt there were at least three empty or rubble-strewn lots. I'd never witnessed that kind of utter devastation.

I had come to the Bay on my way to New Orleans, one of my favorite places in the world. It would be my first trip to the Crescent City since Katrina, and I was eager to see how much the city had changed. While I'd been to New Orleans many times and to the Delta to visit Bubba on the farm in Yazoo City, I'd never seen the Gulf Coast of Mississippi and thought I should. When Katrina came ashore, Bay St. Louis was smack in the middle of its fury, which cut a twenty-mile-wide swath through this part of the coast.

As I drove along the waterfront in the Bay and the neighboring town of Waveland, I wished I'd been able to see them as they had been before the disaster. There were churches that literally had been blown away. An Episcopal parish where only the bell tower remained. A Catholic church broken apart and replaced by white Quonset huts, with a sign in front that read, "Katrina was big, but

God is bigger." Homes missing from their foundations. A private boarding school where the dorms had been destroyed. When I got to Main Street in Old Bay St. Louis, the heart of the town where well-heeled restaurants and quirky shops once lined the streets, I spotted the remnants of what I imagined used to be a popular nightlife destination—a corner watering hole where only part of a brick facade and the frame of a large window remained. A little farther up Main Street, across the street from a municipal building, is a large church building with a ragged, gaping maw where the sanctuary used to be. Draped across the giant hole was a spray-painted drop cloth announcing the three weekly worship times and an arrow pointing to the intact hall next door. Life goes on.

I started to head back to the motel and the Cheesy Gordita Crunch awaiting me at the Taco Bell on Route 90 when I spotted a pristine butter-yellow house with white trim and huge oak trees flanking its entrance. The sign outside read The Sycamore House—a restaurant. It looked like it was open for business. So when I got back to the motel, I found its listing in the Yellow Pages and dialed the number. Voice mail. I left a message asking if they could squeeze in a table for one and giving them my cell phone number. When I hadn't heard back in a half-hour, I got in the car and drove toward the old downtown, figuring it couldn't hurt to just show up at The Sycamore House and take my chances.

As I drove back down Main Street in the Bay, there were people everywhere—kids on scooters, men in loud Hawaiian shirts, and women in casual resort wear strolling along the street with glasses of wine in their hands. For the first time I noticed clusters of small boutiques and art galleries with their lights on, crammed with people doing a brisk business. Parked in front of a shop that sold, among many eclectic items, an assortment of folk art crosses and handmade religious icons (a number of which now adorn the walls of my home in Chicago) was an SUV with a bumper sticker that read, "Jesus Rebuilds." This was the fabled Saturday Night Art Walk, a Bay St. Louis institution that was too stubborn to let something like a natural disaster run it out of town. By the time I turned into The Sycamore House's gravel lot, it was packed, and I couldn't find a spot to park. So I turned onto Main Street and managed to find a parking place a block or two away. The resilient downtown was bustling, despite the mud and puddles and oppressive *Cat on a Hot Tin Roof* swampy humidity.

An effusive Southern welcome greeted me when I walked through The Sycamore House's front door. When I told the hostess that I'd left a voice mail inquiring about a table, she turned to me and said, "You must be Cathleen!" and steered me to a table on the expansive screened-in front porch. I ordered white wine and relaxed, the chilled glass sweating in my hand as I watched the crowds of decidedly artsy-looking folks — I spotted a couple of people with dreadlocks and at least one young woman with a Mohawk — stroll up and down Main Street, laughing and chatting with their neighbors and friends. The artists had returned! Joy had found a way through the wreckage.

A couple of days later, I had a conversation with Jean Larroux, a pastor friend of Bubba's and a native of the Bay who had returned to his hometown after Katrina to start a church called Lagniappe, and he confirmed my impressions of the soul of this town. "This area already understands the celebration of life," he said. "You saw it Saturday night. They take every drop of juice out of the lemon that they can get, and they love it. They love the people, they love the culture, they love art, they love music. They'll be the last ones dancing at the wedding and the first ones to get up and cut up. All of the pieces are in the box. They just don't have the reason—the substantive, foundational reason—to celebrate, which is one of the reasons I'm excited to be here. It's very difficult to take a people who won't celebrate and teach them to. But you can take a people who love to celebrate and give them a greater reason."

Now, for the uninitiated, it's crucial to understand how important food is to the culture in the Bay, New Orleans, and the rest of the Gulf Coast. In these parts, cooking, presenting, and savoring food is a celebration of life itself. That's one of the reasons Jean decided to call his church Lagniappe. It's an old Creole word that means "something extra." It's an unexpected gift. A little bit more. "Down here if you go into a seafood shop and order a pound of shrimp and they put in an extra handful, that's the lagniappe," Jean said. "It's something you can't pay for. Something for nothing. Something for free."

In other words, a lagniappe is getting what you don't deserve?

"Absolutely," Jean said. "In that sense, this area was really primed for grace. It understood the gospel it didn't know. It's like Babette's feast. Too often the church is the gruel sippers who have their faces pressed against the window of the world watching the world celebrate life and they don't get it. When in reality, the father welcomed the prodigal son home in the gospel of Luke, chapter 15, and the world pressed its face against that window to see the celebration of grace."

Back at The Sycamore House, I lingered for a couple of hours over a wonderfully memorable meal. I started with a bowl of watermelon gazpacho. I'd never heard of such a thing. It was like a gustatory festival—sweet and cold and crunchy (raw jicama) and hot (jalapeño peppers). The perfect dish for a sultry Southern evening in the middle of July. I followed the gazpacho with a plate of succulent Gulf shrimp in herbed lime beurre blanc sauce paired with another perfectly chilled glass of white wine. And for dessert—another bowl of the watermelon gazpacho. Then I strolled down the street to do a little shopping for things I absolutely didn't need but had to have anyway.

Sometimes grace is having the strength to persevere through the storm.

Sometimes it's having the guts to rebuild, to take a chance, to follow your nose and your heart rather than your head.

Sometimes grace is finding out that your preconceived notions are dead wrong.

Sometimes it's being surprised by joy.

Sometimes grace is something you can feel even if you can't see it.

And sometimes it's a bowl of watermelon gazpacho when you were expecting Taco Bell.

*Author's Note: A few months after my visit to the Bay, I phoned
The Sycamore House to see if I could get the recipe for that wonderful
gazpacho. Co-owner Michael Eastham, who has run The Sycamore
House with his wife, Stella LeGardeur, since 2002, was kind enough
to tell me I could find it in* We Want Clean Food! *—a book by chef
Ric Orlando of New York's New World Home Cooking Co., with
whom the couple had apprenticed.*

*Here, for your dining pleasure and spiritual edification, is Ric's
recipe:*

Watermelon Gazpacho
(Serves 8)

> 2 pounds red watermelon, seeded and pureed in a blender,
>   rendering about 6 cups watermelon puree (see directions below)
> ½ cup cider vinegar
> ¼ cup water

1 medium cucumber, peeled, seeded, and diced, plus one
    cucumber, peeled and coarsely chopped
½ medium red onion, diced, plus the other half coarsely chopped
4 tablespoons each coarsely chopped basil, spearmint, and cilantro
4 tablespoons red bell pepper, finely diced
½ cup diced jicama
1 teaspoon fresh garlic, minced
1 teaspoon cumin
3 serrano chile peppers or 1 jalapeño chile pepper, sliced into very
    thin rings with seeds included
2 teaspoons salt
3 tablespoons lime juice
½ teaspoon ground pepper

To puree the watermelon, follow these guidelines. This will simplify an otherwise annoying job. Fill your blender about one-third of the way with chunks of watermelon. Add half the vinegar and all of the water. Pulse the blender on low until the watermelon gets caught up and begins to puree. Turn the machine to "liquefy" and run until the watermelon is smooth. Now here's the trick: pour about half of this puree into a large, nonreactive bowl. Use the remaining half of the watermelon puree as the medium to puree more watermelon. Continue until you have pureed enough watermelon to yield 6 cups, plus the cucumber and red onion noted above. If you need to add more liquid, add the remaining vinegar and the lime juice. Do not add more water. In a pinch you can add back some of the pureed watermelon to create enough of a liquid base to finish pureeing the cucumber and onions.

    Mix in all of the other ingredients and stir gently. Chill well.

    Serve ice-cold, garnished with chopped cilantro and a lime wheel.

Where the Streets Have No Names 6

Each time I heard someone call it a "slum," I flinched. That word seemed crass, a pejorative term used to describe something other, something beneath the realm of civil society, a place where suffering and hopelessness reign. But there is no better term to describe Kibera, an enormous tumble of tin shanties, open sewers, and dirt passageways in Nairobi, Kenya, where more than one million people live in abject poverty.

The Slum. Even the people who live in Kibera call it that.

Before I arrived in Africa, the word *slum* conjured vivid images of children with flies in their eyes, women in tattered clothing, and dejected, idle men sitting in the gutter as they pass the time that moves slowly in an unrelenting march of despair. When we turned the corner from embassy row to the mouth of Kibera our first morning in Kenya, the staggering sight put me on my heels. Huts built into the side of a hill and tossed together in a valley as far as I could see. People everywhere—walking, working, and congregating outside their homes and tiny businesses. Scrawny dogs and an occasional cow, goat, or handful of chickens rounded out a tableau unlike anything I'd ever seen.

The British colonial government established Kibera in 1918 as a settlement for Nubian soldiers, a kind of reward for their service to the United Kingdom in World War I and other conflicts. After Kenya won its independence in 1963, the government declared domiciles in Kibera to be illegal, and since 1970 landlords have been renting out property in the slum illegally to far more people than the land can reasonably sustain. Today none of the housing in Kibera, part of which literally is built atop garbage, is technically legal, making it a kind of no-man's-land, beset by pollution and disease. There is no postal service, and the streets, such as they are, have no names. As much as 15 percent of Kibera's population is HIV positive. Most residents have neither electricity nor running water. Crime is rampant, violent conflict among rival ethnic groups erupts almost perennially, flooding is commonplace, and sanitation is primitive at best.

In this part of the world, I am a *mzungu*—the Swahili word for a white person—and mzungus like me are an exotic breed. One woman, who slapped my palm, shook my hand, and grabbed my fingers enthusiastically when we were introduced, later told our guide that I was the first white person she had ever met and touched. If I had any doubts as to the curiosity of my presence in the slum, they were dispelled when I heard children singing while walking in Kibera near a grammar school/orphanage housed in a lopsided corrugated metal building painted an unlikely shade of cheery azure. As I got closer to the school, I realized that the "song" was more of a chant a couple dozen children were yelling over a fence as they ran alongside us, some of them kicking an ersatz soccer ball made from a mound of plastic bags bound together with twine.

"Mzungu! Mzungu! How are you? Mzungu! Mzungu!" they sang at us, giggling and waving.

Apparently, "How are you?" is one of the few English phrases known to most children here who speak Swahili as their primary language, even if they never attend school—and many children in Kibera do not because they cannot afford the uniforms that are compulsory even in Kenyan public schools. A school uniform costs about 1,000 Kenyan shillings. That's about $15. The week before we arrived in Kenya, I had spent more than that on a glass of wine. Never again.

As we walked through the busy streets of Kibera, some people stared at us, sure. But some also invited us into their homes to visit, to tell us their stories, to bless us. It was in these homes that I understood just how mzungu I really am. Everything I saw in Kibera, I saw with mzungu eyes. Everything I heard, I heard with mzungu ears. My challenge was to understand with a heart not colored by my nationality, class, or skin tone.

My husband, Maury, and I had come to Kibera as guests of the Global Alliance for Africa, an American nonprofit that is attempting to help Africans help themselves through microlending and education programs mostly targeting women and their children. Specifically, we were in the slum to meet some women involved in a program called Jikaze — a women's collective that produces yarn, woven rugs, and other handicrafts as a means to support their families and provide the funds their children need to attend school. A typical Jikaze loan is about 5,000 Kenyan shillings, or about $75. The women, who pool their money and share the profits from the handicrafts they sell, are expected to repay the loans within a year or so and also are required to keep immaculate records before they can apply for another, larger loan.

The first time I dropped by the Jikaze Weavers' studio — a neat 8-by-8-foot storefront along Kibera's main commercial thoroughfare — Floice, a mother of four who also cares for two AIDS orphans, was working on a geometric-patterned wool rug. When I admired it, she said she would finish by the next day if I'd like to buy it. We agreed on a price — 2,500 Kenyan shillings. It was only later that it dawned on me: what I bought as a souvenir without giving it a second thought was half of what Floice is hoping to get when her loan comes through.

A soft-spoken woman wearing a T-shirt with a portrait of Mother Teresa and the words "Peace begins with a smile" on it, Floice told me she had faith that she would find a good market for her other rugs and that they would sell. She also said she was hopeful that the loan would come through sooner rather than later, so her life and the lives of her family could change for the better.

A throw rug for me. Food, clothing, and an education for Floice's children.

As we walked the crowded streets of Kibera one afternoon, we stopped to meet several other women involved in Jikaze and other micro-investment projects. There was Mary, who sells corn and always puts an extra handful on top — what folks in New Orleans might call a "lagniappe" — to keep customers coming back. Lillian sells carrots and other vegetables in Toi, Kibera's main open-air market, waking up at 4:00 a.m. to take the bus for an hour in each direction to collect her wares for the day. Margaret, a mother of nine, sews traditional embroidered Kenyan clothing and regularly travels nearly 600-plus miles round-trip by bus to Kampala, Uganda, to buy cloth at the best price she can find. The women's energy and ingenuity were astounding and humbling. They had no time for despair. They are far too busy living.

The flutter and whir of a machine that spins wool into yarn greeted us at another home as we ducked off the street into a short corridor so dark I couldn't see my hand in front of my face. This was Joyce's home. A forty-seven-year-old mother of four daughters, Joyce has been spinning yarn for the Jikaze Weavers' project since 2000. Her husband, Peter, whom she married in 1979 when she was nineteen years old, was a truck driver. Like so many of his compatriots, Peter contracted HIV and died of AIDS in 1997, leaving Joyce with four children under the age of eighteen to care for and little means to support them.

She says her family is blessed because neither she nor any of her children are HIV positive. Still, after Peter's death, the pressure of trying to hold the family together with almost nothing was getting to her. She wasn't sleeping and would pace the floor of her cramped home until the sun came up at the beginning of another day. When she began to have health problems, a doctor told her she needed to find a way to relieve the stress in her life. That's when she started spinning.

"When I'm sitting at the machine, my mind is on the machine and nothing else," Joyce told me. She keeps the machine, large sacks of wool, and the wood-and-steel-wire combs she uses to clean it before spinning it into skeins of one- and two-ply yarn in the corner of her sitting room, behind the lace-doily-covered couch. "When I don't feel like sleeping, I spin until dawn."

She also prays while she works. When she talks to God, Joyce thanks God for pulling her up when she feels like she's slipping down into hopelessness. "I just keep his face before me," she told me, quoting a passage from the biblical book of Psalms: *Fear and trembling have beset me; horror has overwhelmed me. I said, 'Oh, that I had the wings of a dove! I would fly away and be at rest.' ... Evening, morning and noon I cry out in distress, and he hears my voice.*

"When God called my husband home, he has come to me with so much grace," Joyce said over the cry of her grandson in the next room. "Now God is my husband."

Our chaperone in Kibera was a young woman named Josephine. We didn't know much about her the day the van stopped at a busy intersection in the slum to pick her up in front of a cell phone kiosk—one of dozens sprinkled throughout Kibera. (Folks might not have running water or electricity here, but mobile phones are nearly ubiquitous.) Josephine, we learned, was the coordinator of the Jikaze program. Bright and commanding, Josephine led us from home to home, introducing us to the amazing women she works with.

On our last day in Kibera, Josephine took us to a section of the slum we hadn't seen before. Deftly ambling up a narrow passageway, hopping over open streams of sewage that ran between the honeycomb assemblage of apartments and mud huts, she stopped at the threshold of a tidy flat, turned to me, and said, "*Karibu*. You are most welcome. Please come in."

"Whose house is this, Josephine?" I asked.

"This is my home," she said proudly.

I had no idea. My mzungu mind had never considered the possibility that the woman who was helping all these women climb out of stultifying poverty one rug at a time actually lived in Kibera herself.

As we visited with Josephine and her sister, I learned that Josephine had spent her entire life in Kibera. All of her family lives here, including her school-age children. (I didn't know she was a mother either.) She told us her story — about where she had gone to school and university, how she got involved with the Global Alliance for Africa, how she had recently been able to tap into a pirated electrical source and how she was able to pay for a water line to be installed not only for her own use but for her neighbors' use as well.

Had she ever thought of leaving Kibera?

Yes, she said. She has the means to live elsewhere, but she is determined to remain in the slum, where she says God wants her to be. A few years ago, Josephine started taking in orphans from the neighborhood — children who had lost one or both parents to AIDS and had nowhere else to go.

"As long as I have the room, I must give them a home," she said. "That is my commitment."

Surely God lives in Kibera as well. In the slum where the streets have no names, hope springs eternal and grace flows like a river into — and out of — a sea of humanity.

There is but one love of Jesus,
as there is but one person in the poor—Jesus.

—Mother Teresa of Calcutta

Man Hands

The walls of the *Chicago Sun-Times* newsroom are lined with historical black-and-white photos taken by staff photographers over the course of the last century. Their subjects range from the mundane to the magnificent — sports heroes and presidents, icons and everymen, man-made spectaculars and natural disasters. My favorite is a photo of the actress Grace Kelly taken in 1955, a year before she became Princess Grace Grimaldi of Monaco.

In the picture, captured at a then-trendy nightspot called The Pump Room at Chicago's Ambassador East Hotel, Grace is dressed demurely in silk-satin and pearls. In the foreground of the picture, her hands, which are worrying a white cloth handkerchief, are in sharp focus, the closest thing to the observer, thrust out from the frame as if it were in three dimensions rather than two. Each time I pass that photograph, her hands make me stop and stare.

Grace has man hands. They're big and sturdy like Jerry's ill-fated girlfriend in that episode of *Seinfeld* where he's freaked out because she's an absolute beauty except for her big, beefy hands—muscled paws that crack his lobster in half as if it were a peanut shell; big meat hooks that awkwardly, if tenderly, wipe some schmutz from the corner of Jerry's mouth.

Not unlike Jerry Seinfeld, I have a thing about hands. Apart from a person's eyes, hands are the first thing I look at when I meet someone, and I think they're almost as telling as the proverbial window to their souls. Are the hands nervous, with fraught and bitten fingers? Are they long and nimble, as if designed to tickle the keys of a piano or do acrobatics up the neck of a violin? Are they meticulously kempt, with long polished nails and no wayward cuticles or rough patches? Or are they burly and strong, with calluses and scars, the remnants of a lifetime of hard work and adventure?

If a man has wan, delicate hands with—God forbid—longish nails, he may as well also have a pronounced hump, chronic body odor, and a raging heroin addiction, because that's as attractive as he'd ever be to me. One of the sexiest things about my husband is his big, strong, worry-free hands. They're like bear paws, hands he inherited from his father and passed on to his sons, and, most recently, to his newborn grandson, Aidan. I realize judging a man by the size and shape of his hands is sexist at best and most certainly irrational, but it is what it is. It's a natural predilection, the same as my aversion to cilantro and my love of stand-up comedy. Hands say so much, sometimes more than words ever could, and I want to hear what I want to hear — something reassuring and protective and at the same time mindful, gentle, and elegant. That's me. That's what I was looking for in the hands of my true love, the hands that I was lucky enough to convince to hold mine for the remainder of our days on this earth.

Jesus must have had man hands. He was a carpenter, the Bible tells us. I know a few carpenters, and they have great hands, all muscled and worn, with nicks and callused pads from working wood together with hardware and sheer willpower. In my mind, Jesus isn't a slight man with fair hair and eyes who looks as if a strong breeze could knock him down, as he is sometimes depicted in art and film. I see him as sturdy, with a thick frame, powerful legs, and muscular arms. He has a shock of curly black hair and an untrimmed beard, his face tanned and lined from working in the sun. And his hands — hands that pounded nails, sawed lumber, drew in the dirt, and held the children he beckoned to him. Hands that washed his disciples' feet, broke bread for them, and poured their wine. Hands that hauled a heavy cross through the streets of Jerusalem and were later nailed to it. Those were some man hands.

I've heard it said that grace is God reaching God's hands into the world. And the Bible tells us that we are part of the body of Christ, that if we let the Spirit move through us, we can become the hands of Christ on earth. Hands that heal, bless, unite, and love. I'd like to think God's hands are a bit like Grace's man hands — gentle but big, busy, and tough. God's hands are those of a creator — an artist who molded and shaped the universe out of a void, who hewed matter from nothingness.

I keep one of my most prized possessions in the center of our circular dining room table. It's a wood sculpture we bought on our first visit to Nairobi a while back. The story of how we came upon it is one of my favorites to tell.

It was our last day in the Kenyan capital before heading south to Tanzania. After breakfast at the Methodist guesthouse where we were staying, I checked my email and found a note from my dear friend in New York City, the Jesuit priest and author Jim Martin. He'd heard that I was traveling in Kenya and asked me, if time allowed, to please stop by the Jesuit Refugee Service where he lived in the 1990s. During his tenure in Nairobi, Jim opened a shop called the Mikono Centre at the Jesuit compound where refugee artisans sell their wares. Our agenda for the day was pretty full, but we decided to swing by the shop on our way to visit some new friends in Kibera, one of two enormous slums in the city not far from the Jesuit Refugee Service. While we were browsing at Mikono through racks of textiles and paintings depicting African scenes and spiritual tableaus—I purchased a nativity set made entirely from banana leaves—the shop clerk asked if we'd like to see some of the artists at work. One of their most popular artists, she told us, was working on a carving in a building a few yards away.

"His name is Agostino," the clerk said.

Hearing that name felt like a thunderbolt had hit the ground. *Agostino!* Jim had mentioned his name to me with so much love. He'd written about Agostino in his wonderful book *This Our Exile: A Spiritual Journey with the Refugees of East Africa.* Jim had discovered Agostino, a refugee who had fled to Kenya from his native Mozambique, carving rosewood sculptures on a mat outside an office building in downtown Nairobi. Jim invited Agostino to sculpt at the Jesuit compound and sell his pieces at Mikono. He was one of the first artists to do a booming business and gather a following of patrons — a man whose faith, as well as his artistry, had so inspired my friend the priest, and one of the center's great success stories.

I bolted out the door toward the building where the clerk said Agostino was carving. As I turned the corner, there he was, bent over a piece of ebony wood propped up on a broad stump that served as his workbench. He looked exactly as Jim had described him, a bear of a man with liquid eyes, soulful and with a quiet strength, like a living saint.

When I introduced myself and told him I brought greetings from Jim, he beamed.

"Please tell Father Jim that it's a good thing he started Mikono all those years ago," he said. "Now we have children and some of them are in school, and they're in school because of this."

When Agostino said "this," he motioned to the piece he had just finished carving and was beginning to stain with a delicate, long-handled brush.

It was the figure of a small black child pressing his face and hands into the palm of a giant man's hand. Even in its unfinished state, it was breathtaking. We asked Agostino when he thought he would complete the sculpture and told him we would like to buy it and take it home with us. He said he could finish it by that evening. We agreed on a price and told him how glad we were to meet him and how thrilled Jim would be that we had been able to see him.

As we turned to leave, I asked if the sculpture had a name.

"Yes," Agostino said quietly. "It's called 'Hand of God.'"

When we returned that night to collect the Hand of God, Agostino was gone and the sculpture was wrapped in paper and packed carefully in a bag for our travel the next morning. I don't recall how many days later we opened the package to take a better look at the piece, but when we did, we found an added surprise.

On the bottom of the sculpture, next to where he'd signed his name and the date, Agostino had carved a Scripture reference from the 49th chapter of the book of Isaiah. We took out our Bible and looked it up.

This is what it said:

"Can a mother forget the baby at her breast and have no compassion on the child she has borne? Though she may forget, I will not forget you! See, I have engraved you on the palms of my hands."

It doesn't matter which you heard
The holy or the broken Hallelujah

—Leonard Cohen

The Screaming Frenchman 8

Bubba made me promise to visit the Screaming Frenchman, a friend of his from Ole Miss who is a pastor in Bay St. Louis, Mississippi, while I was on a road trip to the post-Katrina Gulf Coast and New Orleans in the summer of 2007.

I almost didn't go. I'm naturally kind of shy — a detriment to someone who fancies herself a journalist, I realize, and a natural inclination I've worked hard to overcome. As I didn't know this fellow from Adam, working up the courage to call on him was a task that, after fifteen hours of driving, I didn't feel up to. But as I had given Bubbs my word, I mustered the energy (psychic and otherwise) and phoned the Frenchman. "Come on over," he said, his voice oozing that ever-gracious down-homey Gulf accent that falls dialectically somewhere between Memphis and Brooklyn.

The Frenchman, whose given name is Jean Larroux, earned the odd nickname while he was a disc jockey at the Ole Miss campus radio station in the early 1990s. (Bubba also refers to him as "the Ragin' Cajun.") All I knew of Jean (pronounced like "gone," not "mean") apart from his funny moniker was that he was a native of Bay St. Louis and had moved back home after Katrina to help with relief work and eventually to start a church in his cataclysm-bedraggled hometown. As I pulled into the muddy driveway of his home near the center of town, I spotted his SUV and a bumper sticker that I took to be an indication I might be about to meet a kindred spirit. It said WWJBD? — as in "What Would Jimmy Buffett Do?" That's my kind of pastor.

Jean is about my age, but with his gray-dappled beard and bespectacled, intensely expressive eyes, he has the look and demeanor of someone with wisdom (and perhaps experience) well beyond his years. We sat down in his living room with cups of coffee and began telling our stories. I was on a trip to see my beloved New Orleans and the Gulf Coast, looking for grace amidst the wreckage left by the hurricane that had ravaged the region almost two years earlier. He had left a lucrative job as an assistant pastor at a well-heeled congregation in Memphis, uprooting his wife and young family to start a church from absolutely nothing in his hometown where something like 90 percent of all the buildings had been blown or washed away when a twenty-eight-foot storm surge made land at high tide on the morning of August 29, 2005. Both endeavors, we agreed, seemed to many people like fools' errands, and we each had been told as much by well-intentioned naysayers before embarking on our respective odysseys.

"I would say that grace is startling," Jean told me as he began retelling the story of how he wound up as pastor of Lagniappe Presbyterian Church, a growing congregation that meets in a glorified metal hangar in Bay St. Louis. "It's just startling. It isn't supposed to work. This wasn't supposed to work."

Jean spent the day before Hurricane Katrina made land in Bay St. Louis trying to convince his mother that she should evacuate from the family home. When you grow up along the coast, hurricanes are commonplace. Occasionally you evacuate, but most of the time you don't. After much cajoling by phone from Memphis, Jean's mother agreed to evacuate and fled her home with little more than the clothes on her back. His aunt and uncle, who also lived in Bay St. Louis, were more stubborn. They decided to stay at home and ride out the storm as they had many times in the past. The day after the storm, Jean arrived in his hometown to find that his cousins had just pulled the bodies of their parents from the wreckage of their destroyed house. So many people along the Gulf Coast of Mississippi and Louisiana have similar tales of unthinkable loss. I find the depth of the sorrows they have to bear impossible to fathom.

Soon thereafter, Jean began coming down from Memphis to Bay St. Louis every weekend. He couldn't get "the Bay," as locals call it, out of his mind. He'd return to Memphis to his beautiful

3,500-square-foot house with a swimming pool in the backyard and to his nice cushy job at the big church with the big office and the executive assistant, but even when he managed to sleep, the Bay crowded his heavy heart. This was about the time he began preaching from the book of Nehemiah in the Hebrew Scriptures (a.k.a. the Old Testament) where in the second chapter the story is told of how the prophet Nehemiah appealed to the Persian king of Susa, whom he served as a cupbearer, to give him a leave of absence so he could return to his homeland, Jerusalem, which had been all but destroyed. "Send me to the city in Judah where my ancestors are buried," Nehemiah pleaded, "so that I can rebuild it." The king agreed and let the prophet go home.

The parallels to what was going on in his own life at the time he was preaching from Nehemiah were not lost on Jean. "It was cool and it was frightening," Jean said. "I tell people all the time it wasn't piety that brought me here. It was really self-preservation because I've read the book of Jonah and I know what happens. I was getting to the Bay one way or the other. Either I could be vomited onto the shore or I could move there." So Jean quit his job in Memphis at the 3,500-member church with the $3.5 million operating budget, and, with his wife, Kim, and their three school-age kids, essentially moved into his mother's FEMA trailer in Bay St. Louis.

When Jean told the powers that be in his denomination that he wanted to start a church in the Bay, they said it couldn't be done. Jean proposed trying to raise $800,000 over six years, and his superiors in the denomination said his goal was honorably ambitious but surely would be impossible. This is where Jean's stubbornness and, perhaps, God's stubborn grace came into play. "My definition of grace would be multifaceted, but part of it would certainly be God's passion for brokenness. He does, he really does love brokenness," Jean told me. "Grace doesn't obsess with ourselves. It obsesses with people and with brokenness. This is a hard place to live, but God is bigger than hard places to live."

At the end of Lagniappe Presbyterian Church's first year, the congregation, peopled by local folks who had lost almost everything — their homes, possessions, livelihoods, and, all too often, loved ones as well — and volunteers from across the country who had come down to the Bay in a steady stream to help the community rebuild, had $1.7 million in the church coffers. The congregation committed to giving away at least 10 percent of all they were given and in that first year was able to write $170,000 in benevolence checks to help struggling, broken people in other parts of the world. In fact, Lagniappe is the single largest donor to a ministry in Colorado that helps sex workers escape the sex-for-sale industry.

From a shed. In the frayed, soggy aftermath of the worst hurricane ever to hit Mississippi. That's nothing short of miraculous.

I met Jean on a Monday. The day before, while he was away on business in another part of the state, I decided to check out Lagniappe's Sunday morning service. It was so familiar. The songs. The people. The message. I was sitting there in the cozy shed, among teams of high schoolers from various locales who had come as volunteers to help build houses in the Bay for a week or two. And in the midst of these lovely people I thought my skin was going to take off without me and run to the car. I left right after the service without saying hello to anyone and went back to my dreary motel room where I sat in a funk for the rest of the day, trying to figure out what had gotten so under my skin and why.

I have a complicated spiritual history. Here's the short version: I was born into a Mass-going Roman Catholic family, but my parents left the church when I was in the fifth grade and joined a Southern Baptist church—yes, in Connecticut. I am an alumnus of Wheaton College—Billy Graham's alma mater in Illinois, not the Seven Sisters school in Massachusetts—and the summer between my junior and senior year of (Christian) high school, I spent a couple of months on a missions trip performing in whiteface as a mime-for-the-Lord on the streets of London's West End. Once I left home for Wheaton, I ended up worshiping variously (and when I could haul my lazy tuckus out of bed) at the nondenominational Bible church next to the college, a Christian hippie commune in inner-city Chicago left over from the Jesus Freak movement of the 1960s, and an artsy-fartsy suburban Episcopal parish that ended up splitting over same-sex issues. My husband of more than a decade likes to describe himself as a "collapsed Catholic," and for more than twenty-five years, I have been a born-again Christian. Groan, I know. But there's really no better term in the current popular lexicon to describe my seminal spiritual experience.

It happened in the summer of 1980 when I was about to turn ten years old. My parents had both had born-again experiences themselves about six months earlier, shortly before our family left the Catholic church—much to the shock and dismay of the rest of our extended Irish and/or Italian Catholic family—and started worshiping in a rented public grade school gymnasium with the Southern Baptists. My mother had told me all about what she'd experienced with God and how I needed to give my heart to Jesus so I could spend eternity with him in heaven and not frying in hell. I was an intellectually stubborn and precocious child, so I didn't just kneel down with her and pray the first time she told me about what was going on with her and Daddy and Jesus. If something similar was going to happen to me, it was going to happen in my own sweet time.

A few months into our family's new spiritual adventure, after hearing many lectures from Mom and sitting through any number of sermons at the Baptist church — each ending with an altar call and an invitation to make Jesus the Lord of my life — I got up from bed late one Sunday night and went downstairs to the den where my mother was watching television. I couldn't sleep, which was unusual for me as a child. I was a champion snoozer. In hindsight I realize something must have been troubling my spirit.

Mom went into the kitchen for a cup of tea and left me alone with the television, which she had tuned to a church service. I don't remember exactly what the preacher said in his impassioned, sweaty sermon, but I do recall three things crystal clearly: The preacher was Jimmy Swaggart; he gave an altar call, inviting the folks in the congregation in front of him and at home in TV land to pray a simple prayer asking Jesus to come into their hearts; and that I prayed that prayer then and there, alone in the den in front of the idiot box.

Seriously. That is precisely how I got "saved." Alone. Watching Jimmy Swaggart on late-night TV. I also spent a painful vacation with my family one summer at Jim and Tammy Faye Bakker's Heritage USA Christian theme park in South Carolina. But that's a whole other book . . .

So I've got some history with this church business, both personal and professional, since, ostensibly, as a religion journalist I go to church for a living. As I took stock of my spiritual journey while sitting in that wretched motel room in Bay St. Louis—it still had a ring of mildew marks a few feet up the wall where the floodwaters had invaded in the first few days after Katrina—I settled on what had bothered me at Lagniappe Church that morning. It was the realization that I once was like those volunteer kids on their missions trip to rebuild the Bay. When I was fifteen I knew what all the rules were. I knew what being a Christian was supposed to mean and, more important, what it was supposed to *look* like. There were lists of things that you couldn't do or say or think and still be a "strong Christian." Life was simpler back then. And I think I was mourning that innocence, long since gone.

Don't drink. Don't smoke. And don't go with boys who do. No sex before marriage. Avoid the evils of feminism and liberal politics. Do not be unequally yoked. The ideal Christian woman is a helpmeet to her husband, lovingly submitting while taking care of hearth and home. Only born-again Christians who have prayed the prayer of salvation are going to heaven; everyone else is misguided or confused or wrong. There is one truth. Be in the world but not of it.

The term *born again* comes from the third chapter of the gospel of John in the New Testament, where Jesus tells Nicodemus, a Pharisee (i.e. a legalistic, self-righteous hypocrite), that he will never make it to heaven, into God's kingdom, unless he is "born again." When Nicodemus nudges Jesus to elaborate, Jesus says, "Flesh gives birth to flesh, but the Spirit gives birth to spirit," making it clear that he was talking about a spiritual rebirth. Jesus explains this born-again concept further by talking about the spirit as a kind of wind you can hear but don't know where it comes from or where it's going—mysterious, elusive, hard to pin down, nearly impossible to describe. These days "born again" is usually employed to describe a very specific experience that follows set rules of engagement: certain words said a certain way and maybe in a certain place in front of certain people, followed by outward manifestations of inward change—certain quantifiable, recognizable changes. The author and theologian Frederick Buechner says some self-described born-again Christians talk about the born-again experience as if it's a recipe for fudge brownies you can look up in the *Fanny Farmer* cookbook—and that if you follow the recipe, you get fudge brownies every time. Buechner argues, quite rightly I believe, that there is no precise recipe of measured spiritual ingredients or that if there is, sometimes you get fudge brownies and sometimes you get a Bundt cake and sometimes you get meat loaf. I think I'm a rhubarb pie with a scoop of pistachio ice cream.

All through college and into my early twenties, I was a good girl, abiding by the rules (mostly), trying desperately to follow the recipe, and worrying the whole time about how I was doing as a Christian—whether I was making the right decisions, thinking the right thoughts, dancing the right steps. Then round about the age of twenty-five, I was tired of being tired of being scared about doing something that, if I deconstruct it honestly, might somehow cost me my salvation and make God love me less. When I understood, in God's grace, that there was nothing—*not a thing*—I could do to make God love me any less or any more, when I understood that there was nothing wrong or right about who I am in God's eyes, that I'm just loved, I started to live. Boldly. Or at least as boldly as I can muster much of the time.

Living boldly (or otherwise, frankly) is messy. That Sunday at Lagniappe, I was ashamed of my messiness. I've heard thousands of "testimonies" of people's redemption stories, amazing tales of having lives bent on destruction turned around and snatched back from the abyss of addiction, out-of-control rage, or terminal self-centeredness. Gang leaders who are now pastors. Single teenage mothers who, through the grace of Jesus, are moral leaders of their communities. Meth heads who have traded a chemical high for a spiritual zenith. But when you surrender your life to God at the age of nine, the conversion story is a lot less dramatic and a whole lot messier. When you make the majority of your big mistakes *after* being born again rather than before, it's not quite as Disney. It's not the story most people — most Christians, for that matter — want to hear or to tell.

When I told Jean, a veritable stranger, all of this in his living room the next day, he nodded knowingly and took out a pack of cigarettes. "I'm so addicted to the verdicts of men. I mean, I *really* am," Jean said, lighting one. "I think the great temptation for ministers is to talk about our sin in neatly packaged sermon illustrations so I can clean it up and sterilize it to the place where it's actually a subtle illustration of my victorious application of Jesus rather than a true illustration of the fact that I'm an asshole." This made me laugh out loud, settle in, and urge him to continue. "I mean, I come into work and I've got all this stuff going on and I snap at somebody and I'm just a real, live asshole. And grace in that moment, you can't neatly package. It's somebody throwing their arms around you and saying, 'I love you, but you are an asshole.'"

Yes, but you're my *asshole,* I envision God saying.

"Grace doesn't deny my assholeness," Jean said. (I immediately had the urge to put that on a T-shirt.) "Grace can't be amazing until your sin is amazing. You've got to get in that place where you can be startled by it, because if you do everything right, you don't deserve it."

And that's just not interesting.

"It's just not *true!*" Jean said with the kind of passion that helped me understand why someone might have decided to call him the Screaming Frenchman. He tells me the story of the time not long after he'd relocated to the Bay when he phoned one of his pastor friends to ask for prayer and guidance. "I had just a bunch of crap going on down here and I said, 'Man, pray for me. I'm trying to quit smoking.' And his exact response was, 'Do you hate yourself? Why would you do that? Your life is hell right now. You *ought* to smoke!' And I was like, 'I love you. Thank you.'"

Which is what I wanted to say to Jean at that point in the conversation, sitting there in his living room, absolutely startled by grace, which, Jean explained, is like Narnia from C. S. Lewis's allegorical fantasy books. "It's all thawing and it's all coming to life," he said. "The rivers are flowing and everything is alive, and the grace is real and everything is real, but there continually are new places. The place God has had me in the last few years is taking me to the places in Narnia where I realize it's OK not to be OK. The law could have just beat my ass telling me to love people, and grace took me by the hand and romanced me to Bay St. Louis and said, 'Just love people.'"

Holy crap. I was dying, overcome with how much sense, the deep-down kind of sense that curls your toes, Jean was making. I was overwhelmed by how much I needed to hear someone say it, right there, right then, in that kind of language. I had come to the Bay looking for grace, thinking I'd find it in tales of the reconstruction. I had no idea the rebirth I'd discover would be my own.

I had to hit the road to make it to New Orleans in time to join my husband, who was flying in to meet me. Jean and I made plans to meet in New Orleans with our spouses some day soon. I didn't want to say good-bye, I just wanted to stay with the Screaming Frenchman, listening to him shout into the wind.

Before I left, Jean asked if he could pray for me. Together, on his back porch, his cigarette smoke rising like incense to the heavens, we spoke to the God of grace we both are so grateful to know up close and personal. It may be the most beautiful prayer I've ever heard.

Jesus, for some reason you've given us another day, and you've set us in Narnia. There are people who still think it's frozen, and there are people who are longing to be thawed but don't know it. God, I pray that what you've called us to do would be the subversive work of the kingdom, that we would help participate in the melting of Narnia, and that people would come alive and would drink and dance and sing and just celebrate life in ways that are so marvelous that the world would press its face against the glass and see the redeemed celebrate life.

Amen.

I remained, lost in oblivion;
My face I reclined on the Beloved.
All ceased and I abandoned myself,
Leaving my cares forgotten among the lilies.

—Saint John of the Cross

Knotted Celt

9

Howling wind whipped my long, unruly hair in penitent lashes across my face as I stood in the rain, staring at the churning sea at the northernmost point of Ireland. This place, Malin Head in County Donegal, for some mysterious or mystical reason—perhaps because it is such a broody, dramatic place, or maybe it's got something to do with ancestry, or both—is the spot I love most in the world.

It is a wild land, the kind of place where myths are born, where giants and saints might come bounding over the next hillock followed by a troupe of little people or a herd of magical sheep.

Whatever the reason, I feel at home here and have returned time and again over the last fifteen years, drawn to stand on its rocky cliffs like water to the shore.

At the very tip of Malin Head is Banbha's Crown, named for one of the legendary goddess-queens of Ireland. Here stands a tower that from a distance looks as if it might be the ruins of a castle fort but is actually a signal tower built in 1802 by the British and used during World War II — along with several small huts and the word EIRE (one of Ireland's ancient names) spelled out in a meadow along the cliff in letters formed by thousands of white rocks piled together — as a navigational and lookout point to protect Ireland's neutrality. (Ireland was a neutral nation during the war.) A bit farther down, tucked into the cliffs where the Atlantic roars against the rocky land, is the Wee House of Malin, a cave that is said to have been the hermitage of St. Muirdealach. According to lore, no matter how many people entered St. Muirdealach's cave, there was always room for more.

I first came to Malin Head when I was twenty-three years old, just prior to beginning my first year of graduate work at seminary. It was my first trip to Ireland, the island my grandmother Nell left in the early 1920s when she was about the same age on a ship bound for Ellis Island and a new life in America. In fact, I was the first member of the family to return to Ireland since she had left. I never knew Nell. She died giving birth to her fourth child when my mother, Helen (named after her mother), was three years old. Still, Nell had been a palpable presence in my world, precisely, I think, because of her absence from my life and, more important, from my mother's. My grandmother was one of twenty-one children born to my great-grandfather, who was married twice. His first wife had eleven children before she died, and his second, my great-grandmother, bore another ten. As a result, I have loads of family left in Ireland, and I took that first trip to the ancestral homeland, in part, to find them and reconnect.

That first journey to Ireland was one of many firsts. The first member of my family to come "home" from America. The first trip I'd ever taken alone. The first time I'd gone by myself to dinner in a restaurant, had a drink alone in a pub, and ventured out solo to a nightclub to dance. My first experience driving on the left side of the road in a car with its steering wheel on the right. I spent three weeks in Ireland and would go whole days without speaking to another soul except the kindly proprietors of the bed-and-breakfasts where I stayed each night. It was the first time I'd spent that much time alone in my life, and it was at times harrowing, alone with my thoughts for hours at a time as I drove through some of the most spectacular scenery I'd ever seen before or since. I found this island breathtakingly beautiful, so much so that as I motored through the west of Ireland, I regularly had to pull over to the side of the road to weep.

"Grace to me is a little bit of extra help when you're feeling stuck or doomed or, probably, hopefully, out of good ideas on how to save yourself, and how to salvage the situation or the friendship or the whatever it is," Anne Lamott once told me. "I wish it was accompanied by harp music so you could know that's what was happening, but for me it's that extra pause or that extra breath or that extra minute's patience against all odds." On that first trip to Ireland, grace — the kick-in-the-pants, clarifying, cosmic-pause-button kind of grace — didn't just have a harp. It had an entire soundtrack, a two-volume set of traditional and contemporary

Irish music called "Bringing It All Back Home." I listened to it nonstop for three weeks and am on my third copy of it now, fifteen years later. Certain songs remind me distinctly of particular places in Ireland. Mary Black's gorgeous ballad "No Frontiers" — *And heaven has its way / Heaven knows no frontiers* — is a back road on the outskirts of my grandmother's village where the ruins of our tiny ancestral home can be glimpsed from inside their cage of ivy and brambles. "Oileán/Island," a seven-minute instrumental performed by pianist Mícheál ÓSúilleabháin and the Irish Chamber Orchestra is a sunset drive from the Cliffs of Moher to the seaside town of Doolin in County Clare. And "Equinox," a haunting instrumental by Davy Spillane, the famous Irish uilleann piper and low whistle player, is the long, serpentine approach to the tip of Malin Head.

What is it about this place that tugs at my soul, pulling at it like a spiritual magnet?

It can't be ancestral ties, as my grandmother surely never set foot here. Nell was from a village in the middle of Ireland, a border town in County Cavan's lake district called Ballyjamesduff (where a couple dozen of my cousins still live) about 100 miles from Malin Head. Still, there is a mystifying connection here for me. Even on that first visit I felt like I'd been here before, as if part of my spirit resides in this wild land.

Of such places, in his poem "In Transit," W. H. Auden described that kind of bond between person and place far more eloquently than I could. He wrote:

> *Somewhere are places where we have really been, dear spaces*
> *Of our deeds and faces, scenes we remember*
> *As unchanging because there we changed*

When I stand in Banbha's Crown, the link I feel to its physical space is rooted in the association it has for me with change, be it a powerful transformation that has just occurred or one about to transpire. It's a place where I've faced down my fears (temporal and eternal) and had visions of the future, good and bad. The first time I visited Malin Head, I spent a couple of hours strolling along the cliffs, gathering white stones, as is the custom, to spell out my initials and those of the young man I was in love with at the time and presumed I would marry one day in the not-too-distant future. I overcame a lifelong fear of heights in this place because in order to really experience it in all its drama and power you have to get close to the edge and look down where a gaping maw in the cliffs is hewn out by crashing whitecaps of a slate blue sea. You have to get close to the edge to be truly at the farthest point north. You have to get close to the edge to be at the end of the earth, at the top of the world, at the verge of oblivion where the land drops off into the water and whatever lies beyond it.

The second time I made the trek to Malin Head, I was with the not-so-young man I fell in love with and married four years later. We were on our honeymoon, and I had a fierce head cold that would, the next day, turn into a vicious bronchial infection and send me to the emergency room of a hospital in Derry, Northern Ireland. I made the hike down to the meadow on the cliffs with an asthma inhaler in one hand and a fistful of tissues in the other, my new husband keeping a watchful eye on me as I scrambled unsteadily over the rocks. I remember how fearless my husband was that day on the cliffs, how unafraid he was of the cliff's edge, of edges in general. It could be a false recovered memory, but I seem to recall him lying on his stomach and sticking his head over the edge of the cliff into a particularly dramatic abyss called "Hell's Hole" and laughing as the Atlantic jettisoned sea spray from the stony breach. I remember how dashing and handsome he looked, how in love with him I was and still am, even though I was afraid of the unknown, of what might happen next in the life we had just begun together, as much as I was afraid of him being blown off the cliff by the gales that blow through Banbha's Crown.

It is said that Malin Head is the sunniest spot in all of Ireland — nothing to cast a shadow, I suppose. On this overcast day, there is no sun. But there is clarity.

I wonder what has this Celt knotted, what I am afraid of this time. As always, it is a certain fear of the unknown, of change and evolution. Of what I have become in the fifteen years since I first stood in this spot. Of what I will be thinking about fifteen years from now. If I will be standing still, taking stock of the past, gracespotting — and what I might find if I do.

I took my most recent trip to Malin Head to try to figure out in my head what my heart already knew — what ties me to this mystical place. I am alone now in Banbha's Crown. The only other visitors — a couple of Irish pensioners eating lunch and reading the tabloid papers in their car — have left. I can hear the wind before I feel it. And the roar of the ocean. And the call of the corncrakes and gannets. Bathed not in sunshine or rain, but in a shower of grace.

Alone at the edge.

A soundtrack playing in my mind.

Looking.

Longing.

Ready.

For whatever comes next.

One is changed by what one loves.

—Joseph Brodsky

Sin Boldly

10

It's Sunday morning and I am hungover.

I should be in church somewhere, I suppose, but I'm not. Instead I am hiding under the covers, vaguely nauseated, waiting for the four ibuprofen I gobbled down a few minutes ago to kick in and trying to rehydrate after a night of drinking too much wine with a rabbi, his wife, my husband, and his sister, Madonna. (Not *that* Madonna, but that really is her given name, and yes, I realize last night's dinner guest list has the makings of a pretty good joke.)

I should not have had that fourth glass of wine, or the cigarette chaser.

I should have gotten up and at least gone to the gym, if not that nice morning meditation session at the yoga center, or the sung Eucharist at Grace Episcopal, or the 11:00 a.m. if-you're-happy-and-you-know-it evangelical worship service at the nondenominational joint a few blocks away.

I should be more disciplined, more temperate, more grown-up. I should be more Christian, I suppose, whatever that means.

And I should know what that means.

As Al Franken's old *Saturday Night Live* character Stuart Smalley might say, I'm *shoulding* all over myself.

I am spending Sunday morning hunched miserably in front of the computer instead of seeking forgiveness for my sins on my knees in front of an altar. All the while, the words of that U2 song "In a Little While" play in my mind on a loop.

In a little while, this hurt will hurt no more . . .

Bono has said he wrote the song about a hangover. But I wonder whether he meant a physical hangover after a long night of what the Irish call *craic*, or something more eternal, existential, fundamental.

The oenophilia-induced yuck I'm battling this morning pales in comparison to the *spiritual* hangover I've got going. This most recent bout has been lurking around for a week, and no amount of painkillers and iced green tea will make it go away.

"I'm a total disaster," I tell my husband, skulking into the living room and draping myself dramatically across the hassock.

"How so?" he asks, barely looking up from his Sudoku.

"In every way," I mumble.

"No, honey, I don't think so," he says.

Am too, I say in my head and shuffle back, dejected, to my dimly lit home office.

A certified disaster. Card-carrying member of the House of Pain. The runt of the spiritual litter. I even have the documentation to prove it, a petition of sorts — several hundred angry emails sent to me during the last week by a phalanx of self-identified Christians with their undies in a bundle about a column I wrote.

This is far from the first time I've received hate mail, and I'm sure it won't be the last. And it's also not the first time the hate mail — vitriolic and sometimes downright vulgar invectives impugning my character (spiritual and otherwise) — has come from my brothers and sisters in Christ. A few years back, when I wrote about a friend of mine who is culturally Jewish, begrudgingly atheistic, and honestly flummoxed by what she sees as the spiritual disconnect between President George W. Bush's professed faith and his public policy, political and religious conservatives lambasted me for weeks as a liberal (which, by the way is not an insult), a heretic, an embarrassment, and a fool.

This time around, the object of the complainants' disaffection was a column I wrote a few days after the death of the Rev. Jerry Falwell on May 15, 2007. I'd written:

> When doctors pronounced the Rev. Jerry Laymon Falwell Sr. dead at 12:40 p.m. Eastern Standard Time on Tuesday, I was sitting in the departures lounge of the Key West airport in Florida with a dozen other journalists who had just attended a three-day conference on religion and politics.
>
> As word spread — a producer for National Public Radio got the first call — my colleagues scrambled to their cell phones, BlackBerrys, and laptops in preparation to write stories and, as was the case with a few, give live radio interviews about the impact of the Rev. Falwell's death.

Knowing I didn't have a deadline to meet that day, my first thoughts were not of what to say or write.

In fact, my very first thought upon hearing of the Rev. Falwell's passing was one word: Good.

And I didn't mean "good" in a "oh good, he's gone home to be with the Lord" kind of way. I meant "good" as in "ding-dong, the witch is dead."

But that thought — good riddance, I suppose — was not meant to be cruel or malicious. After all, the faith that the Rev. Falwell and I share teaches us that he was, at that moment, in a far better place, with Jesus in heaven, and not roasting on a spit in hell's kitchen.

By shrugging off his mortal coil, the Rev. Falwell had ceased to suffer the pain of humanity. Still, I'm not particularly proud of my knee-jerk reaction. But there it is.

My first thought was not sympathy for his grieving family and friends, nor empathy for the students at Liberty University who surely were shocked by the sudden passing of the school's founder in his office on campus. I didn't think of the Rev. Falwell's best intentions, nor about what good he might have contributed to the world during his nearly seventy-four years on this earth. That came much later.

My initial reaction to the Rev. Falwell's death was, and remains, relief — not unlike the ease I felt when a particularly nasty bully who used to spit at me on the playground and threaten to beat me up after school moved to another town.

The Rev. Falwell was a spiritual bully. He was the Tony Soprano to Pat Robertson's Paulie Walnuts.

People who know both of us have told me over the years that we'd probably have liked each other, the Rev. Falwell and I, that he was an affable, almost jolly man, not nearly as smug and awful as his public persona made him out to be.

I'm sure, were he real, Tony Soprano also would make a

charming dinner companion, sharing his lasagna and a nice bottle of Orvieto while telling great stories and asking how your grandmother's doing in the home. And then he'd have you whacked and thrown over the side of his deep-sea fishing boat. But he'd send flowers to the funeral.

After all, as another famous Christian leader once told me by way of explaining how some evangelicals turn on each other (never mind their perceived enemies):

"We shoot our own."

I will not miss the Rev. Falwell, though the faith he and I share assures me we'll have plenty of time to catch up as we spend eternity together in God's house of many mansions.

Who knows whether, at this moment, the Rev. Falwell is polishing one of the many crowns he's stored up in heaven from his good work for the kingdom on earth, or is on day three of his seminar with Jesus about what the gospel really means and how the reverend had royally screwed up the message? Only God is privy to that kind of insight.

And if there's one thing I learned from the Rev. Falwell's example, it was to heed Jesus' warning to "judge not."

I won't miss having to apologize for the insensitive, mean-spirited, sometimes downright hateful things the Rev. Falwell said in the name of Christ. I won't miss having to explain that not all evangelicals are like the Rev. Falwell, that not all of us are that self-righteous, judgmental, and holier-than-thou.

The Rev. Falwell's absence from this realm will mean one less voice telling my gay and lesbian friends that they are somehow less loved by God, that AIDS is God's wrath, that they are to blame for calamities such as 9/11 or Katrina. I really won't miss the pain in my friends' eyes when they ask me how the Rev. Falwell and I could both be Christians but be so different from each other.

I will not miss seeing him on CNN, pontificating about what

God's intention was in allowing and/or causing the latest natural disaster, massacre, plague, famine, or terrorist attack.

I will not miss the Rev. Falwell's voice or point of view.

But at the same time, I cannot dismiss the good he somehow managed to accomplish, despite the pain he inflicted. Lives were changed for the better by his ministry, his college, and the flip side of the endeavors he made in Jesus' name.

There is no denying that some people came to know a loving God through the efforts of the Rev. Falwell. I'm not arrogant enough to presume that God can't work through any means available.

Surely the Rev. Falwell was a cracked vessel for the Spirit of God, but aren't we all?

Now he is enjoying his eternal reward.

May he rest in peace.

And may grace fill his absence.

The response this column elicited from many self-identified Christian readers was anything but grace-filled. In short, I got flamed.

A typical email started with the subject line, "Rev. Falwell is not a 'witch,'" (I never said he was, of course), and went on to demand my resignation and/or public humiliation/apology, as well as questioning the validity of my professed faith. Some called me a Satanist, a lesbian, a whore, a bitch, a liar, disgusting, shameful, an embarrassment to my alma mater, an embarrassment to my "once noble profession," an ally of (gasp!) homosexuals and feminists and abortionists, a "fake Christian," and a host of other mean, nasty, ugly things that would give my publisher fits if I attempted to reproduce them in these pages. Many of the emailers accused me of grave dancing, saying that I was full of hate. Still others insisted that I would get what was coming to me on Judgment Day, that no one would miss me (either) when I'm dead, that clearly I am lost (not found), and that they are praying for the disposition of my eternal soul. A few expressed all of these sentiments at once in the same email and signed it, "in His service," or "yours in Christ."

(The crashing sound you just heard was Jesus banging his head against the wall in his office.)

A decade of writing for the mainstream media about all things religious has conditioned me to flinch at emails and letters that begin with the words "As a Christian ..." because what often follows this qualifying phrase/divine imprimatur is something so small-minded, wrongheaded, self-righteous, and arrogant that it would make the Son of God want to start doing Jager shots and hurl his sandals at you. As a Christian, they know the truth. As a Christian, they are in a position to tell me when I am wrong (and it's most of the time). As a Christian, they are superior to me — morally, theologically, and spiritually. As a Christian, they have my best interests at heart and want to lead me back to the path of righteousness. As a Christian, they are insulted by what I've said or thought. As a Christian, they say I give Christians a bad name. As a Christian, they say I should know better. As a Christian, they're sure I'm way too liberal. As a Christian, they're certain I can't write what I write and be one too. And so on.

What was it Jesus said in the thirteenth chapter of the gospel of John in the New Testament? "By this everyone will know that you are my disciples, if you love one another." Love. Hostility. Same difference, no?

I know—oh, Lord, do I know—that the fastest way to get into trouble spiritually is to look to other Christians as an example for how to live a life of faith rather than looking to Jesus himself. The Bible tells us that Jesus was perfect and always made the right decisions. His followers? Not so much. Still, as the nineteenth-century American evangelist Dwight Moody once said, "Of one hundred men, one will read the Bible; the ninety-nine will read the Christian." What many of the proverbial ninety-nine see when they read most Christians today doesn't look much like the Jesus of the Bible, who was all about revolutionary inclusiveness, radical love, and audacious grace.

We're so worried about the legal details of crossing doctrinal t's and dotting sociopolitical i's that we miss the big picture. The love picture. The one thing Jesus was really clear about: LOVE. If we could just get that one thing down, I believe the details would take care of themselves.

To get back to the late Rev. Falwell and my musings on his death: Don't speak ill of the dead. That doesn't come from the Bible. It comes from common courtesy. I know this. And I honestly didn't intend what I wrote to give the appearance of grave dancing. I wasn't angry or bitter when I wrote what I wrote. I was trying to be sensitive and honest about what I was feeling, to speak the truth in love, as they say. And, yes, *as a Christian.*

Despite all the grief I've received for it, I still think that column is one of the best I've written. Even on this difficult Sunday morning.

So why the hangover?

One of my favorite theological quotes adorns a couple of pint glasses in my kitchen: "Sin Boldly." Martin Luther, that great theological hoodlum and father of Protestantism, is the one who wrote it in a letter to his best friend, Phillip Melanchthon, while hiding in Germany's empty Wartburg castle in 1521, shortly after the Roman Catholic hierarchy put Luther on trial for heresy at a place called Worms.

Luther wrote the letter during a period in the history of Christianity when the established church, i.e., the Roman Catholic Church, had its priorities all out of whack. It was a sin to drink the wine during the sacrament of what is commonly called "Communion," but it was perfectly fine to purchase the alleged forgiveness of sins in the form of indulgences, meted out by priests and bishops. It was considered sinful for clergy to marry and nearly — if not quite — sinful for average Christians (those not ordained by the church) to read Scripture for themselves.

For those who disagreed, like Luther, it was a nervous time. Inquisitors from Rome were menacing anyone who didn't march in lockstep with the powers that be, and many martyrs were made. Dissenters were threatened with their lives, both temporal and eternal. In the midst of all of that chaos, perhaps the direst threat to the faith, as Luther saw it, was missing the theological forest for the trees. Many believers were so consumed with what was and was not a sin — the minutiae and mundane — that they were missing the central message of the gospel: that it is by grace that we are saved, through faith, and not by anything we do or don't do otherwise.

Actually, to put Luther's sexy quote in context (if anything about Lutheranism can be considered sexy, surely it has to be this nearly 500-year-old theological sound bite), what he said in that famous letter to his skittish friend Melanchthon was this:

If you are a preacher of Grace, then preach a true, not a fictitious grace; if grace is true, you must bear a true and not a fictitious sin. God does not save people who are only fictitious sinners. Be a sinner and sin boldly, but believe and rejoice in Christ even more boldly. For he is victorious over sin, death, and the world. As long as we are here we have to sin. This life is not the dwelling place of righteousness but, as Peter says, we look for a new heavens and a new earth in which righteousness dwells. . . . Pray boldly — you too are a mighty sinner.

Sin boldly.
Believe boldly.
Rejoice boldly.
Pray boldly.

Luther's "sin boldly" was not a get-out-of-jail-free card urging us to trespass with abandon because we are covered by grace. That would be too easy. But it's just as easy to misinterpret Scripture. As a journalist, I am all too aware of how easy it is to take someone's words and make them mean something the speaker never intended them to mean. So I went to a friend of mine who knows more about Martin Luther than anyone else I know: Martin Marty, the prolific author, theologian, and perhaps the greatest living historian of American religion. He also happens to be a Lutheran and the author of a biography about Luther.

" 'Sin boldly' doesn't mean 'don't worry about God's law,' " Marty assured me. "At the same time, Luther remembered his own past in the monastery, where there were not many opportunities to 'sin,' but where he sometimes confessed for six hours."

While such scrupulosity in the examination of one's soul,

actions, and intentions can be an honorable endeavor, more often than not it morphs into a kind of self-centeredness. "Get over it," Luther says, according to Marty. The father of Protestantism worried that efforts to become hyperpious would lead "to the development of folks like Garrison Keillor's Lutheran Norwegian bachelor farmers—timid, wan, etc. In this case he had in mind his colleague and best friend Philip Melanchthon, who was preoccupied with little 'do I dare?' sins. No, 'SIN BOLDLY!'"

Luther loved paradoxical language and his note to Melanchthon was full of it, Marty says. The purpose of the "sin boldly" statement really was to highlight what came next. "It is the rest of the three lines that he wanted to accent: about fervency of belief and enjoyment of grace. Throughout his career, he did what he could to keep us from having dull moments."

In other words, if you're going to screw up, at least do it with feeling.

Sin boldly.

Believe in grace even more boldly.

Love without limits.

Live this life.

Still, when faced with a chorus of my co-religionists booing and throwing rotten tomatoes, I had second thoughts about the Falwell column. Did I do the right thing? Doubts lingered like the throbbing headache from too much wine.

That's when I got the message. An email, actually, from someone I'd never met and probably never will. I'll call her Michelle.

Good afternoon, Cathleen,

*I was taken to your column by a link I hit on the Internet.
I was taken aback by how fast I grew to like you as a columnist.
It seems so many times on the media Christians are portrayed as
the Pat Robertson and the Jerry Falwell types when that is not the
Christianity I know at all. What I believe is that GOD is Love.
I believe very strongly in Matthew 22:37 – 40, that is, to love him
and each other. I am a Transsexual, and I hate it when people say,
"God would have made you a girl if HE wanted you that way."
What, do you think HE made a mistake? No! GOD does not make
mistakes. He created me just as I am, divinely, just as he creates
everyone divinely. Why is it people think so small when it comes
to GOD? I believe I was created this way for a reason. It was the
knowledge that GOD always knew who I was and loved me just as
I was that kept me alive when I wanted to end it all. It really hurts
when I see other Christians turning on me because I don't fit into
their neat box of who I should be. Thanks for your columns; I will
look forward to reading more. God bless you.*

> *In Christian Love,*
> *Michelle*

Michelle is the reason I wrote what I wrote. Michelle is the
reason I do what I do. Her kind note helped me remember that
my audience is not the big, bellicose voices of God's professional
bloviators. If they want to read over the shoulders of the marginal-
ized, hurting, scared, ostracized, wounded rest of us, more power
to them. But they're not the point. Michelle is.

I once asked Anne Lamott if she believed we can be grace for
other people. She said she likes to think that we can "hold space" for
one another, kind of like the people who fill seats at the Academy

Awards ceremony when movie stars have to pee or step outside to sneak a nervous cigarette.

"When we stop trying to fix and control other people, or to try to love them into behaving the way we want them to, then all sorts of things start to happen," Annie told me. "When we give up fixing, controlling, and thinking our ideas are good ones, then the plates of the earth start to shift."

Holding space for people is sometimes an active endeavor — speaking up for those who are unable for one reason or another to find their own voice, intervening to stop suffering or injustice, becoming a miracle for someone else. But mostly, Annie says, we are grace for one another when we are simply present. To sit quietly for ten minutes and listen without offering opinions or advice or positions or judgments is profoundly refreshing.

Often grace is as simple as offering a cold glass of water to someone feeling "twitterpated and exhausted," Annie says.

Fresh air and a tall glass of cool water also work wonders for a hangover.

Grace is Christianity's best gift to the world, a spiritual nova in our midst exerting a force stronger than vengeance, stronger than racism, stronger than hate. Sadly, to a world desperate for this grace the church sometimes presents one more form of ungrace. Too often we more resemble the grim folks who gather to eat boiled bread than those who have just partaken of Babette's feast.

—Philip Yancey

Oh, Henry

11

Maury and I spent the first nine years of our marriage living in a two-bedroom flat on the second floor of a Victorian house in the "historic district" of a village just west of the Chicago city limits. When we moved in, the wood floors had just been refinished, there was fresh paint on the walls, and the anachronistic dishwasherless kitchen with its ancient porcelain-topped stove that wouldn't get hotter than 375 degrees (and then only after we'd lit it with a match—risking life, eyebrows, and arm hair—cranked it up to 500 degrees on the dial, and waited an hour for something to happen) seemed quaint.

The flat looked out on a couple of maple trees and with its east-west windows, was bathed in gorgeous amber and ocher light every afternoon. It was cozy, warm, and inviting. We loved the place. That is, for about the first seven years. Then charming and quaint started to morph into shabby and annoying. It was drafty. The floors had lost their luster. The paint was chipping. We couldn't fit a turkey big enough for our expanding family in the tiny oven, and if Maury — the designated dishwasher — had to face another sink full of pots and pans, I thought he might lose his mind.

So we began to search for a new home with more room, better amenities, central air-conditioning, and a kitchen designed on this side of 1920. We looked and looked and looked. For two years. We must have seen every three-bedroom flat and condominium in our village. But nothing was better — bigger, cozier, or as ideally located — than our old Victorian, which, like some women of a certain age, looked her best only in soft lighting.

In the summer of 2006, in the midst of a hellish heat wave, Maury saw a listing for a three-bedroom townhouse four blocks west of what we had come to call "the Gray Lady." I'm not a big fan of townhouses, but it had air-conditioning and two floors, so I agreed to take a look. At the time, a handful of medical students were living in it, and suffice it to say, their aesthetic was different than mine. For instance, I enjoy opening the blinds to give my home less of a cavelike ambiance. I also prefer to scrub the shower occasionally and vacuum more than once a year. As soon as we walked in, I wanted to turn around and walk out. But Maury had strolled straight through the high-ceilinged living room with tall windows and a fireplace and into the kitchen. A big(ger) kitchen with an island and ... be still my heart ... a dishwasher. I kid you not: Maury started to cry.

We took our time looking the place over, and I was beginning to think it had some possibilities, at least as a raw space. But it hadn't won me over. While Maury stood gawking wantonly at the kitchen, I headed through the den and out the back door to the fenced-in garden. That's when I saw it—an enormous mulberry tree stretching a thick canopy of branches over the expansive yard like a bract umbrella. It was a male mulberry, so there were no sticky black berries all over the place. Pretty English ivy covered the split-rail fence on one side of the yard and crawled up the trunk of the tree. It was so quiet and still back there, under the mulberry. I knew then that I could live with the interior of the townhouse, but I couldn't live without that tree.

We moved in two weeks later and named the tree "Henry."

My whole life I've heard people talk about their home as being a sanctuary, the place where they feel the most comfortable, a shelter in the storm, a reflection of who they are. And I suppose I'd felt that way about some of the places I've lived before. Anywhere Maury is, is home to me, and I love being there with him, wherever *there* may be. But in this new space I grasped for the first time the sense that home is a sacred space—sacred in a Joseph Campbell kind of way. "Your sacred space is where you can find yourself again and again," Campbell, the American mythologist, said.

In our new home, with its different contours and light and hush, I've found myself in ways I'd never expected. I want to be at home in this sacred space of ours more than anywhere else in the world. And for someone with chronic wanderlust, that's pretty miraculous.

Speaking of miraculous, thanks to the modern miracle of

wireless Internet access, I am able to work outside in the warm summer mornings at a picnic table under Henry's verdant marquee or on cool autumn afternoons on a carpet of canary yellow leaves while the mulberry tree's graceful, bare limbs make a mosaic of the sky. That first spring in our new home, for the first time in my adult life, I spent more time outside than indoors. For more than twenty years, I'd passed each spring inside a classroom or an office, experiencing the change of seasons under the pallid glower of fluorescent lights. I planted a garden for the first time since I was a child, and as I sat at the patio table typing on my laptop under Henry's umbrella of grace, I could practically see the young tomatoes-to-be perking up in the sun and the morning-glory vines creeping up the stakes along the fence. Like magic.

Gardening is an inherently hopeful endeavor. You put the seeds or the seedlings in the ground, water them, and watch, hoping that leaves will leaf, flowers will blossom, and fruit will appear sometime in the future. This got me thinking about one of my beloved college professors, Rolland Hein, now emeritus professor of literature at Wheaton College. Hein was, to my mind, all tweed and Faulkner until one summer evening more years ago than I care to mention, when I saw the august professor dressed in a gardener's jumpsuit, wild-haired and sweating as he worked in his immense garden that abutted a friend's yard in Wheaton.

I was shocked to see Hein in a setting so viscerally and dramatically different from the austere classrooms at Blanchard Hall—kind of like a third-grader who runs into her teacher at the supermarket. I was simultaneously kerfuffled and intrigued by Hein's agrarian alter ego. In light of my new preoccupation with all things outdoorsy/gardeningy, I looked up the professor and asked if I could come for a visit. Walking the grounds of his home an hour west of Chicago, I was astounded at the vigor with which he approaches gardening. It is not a hobby for Hein. Gardening is a passion.

"It would be difficult to live without it," Hein told me, as we walked through one of four huge gardens that flank his home. While we strolled and chatted, catching up after more than fifteen years, the professor pointed out beds of daylilies, Russian sage, and Oriental poppies. More than 3,000 daffodils danced across his massive garden that also includes apple, plum, and white peach trees; a grape arbor; and unplanted beds awaiting the arrival of hundreds of dahlias — his specialty. My grandfather grew dahlias, and in his honor my bridesmaids carried bouquets of them in shades of chocolate and deep burgundy at our wedding in 1997.

Dahlias are the professor's favorite flower. He's something of an expert at cultivating the blossoms he calls "the king of flowers." What is it about these bushy blooms that arrive in late summer, even though in February he begins readying in his basement the tubers for planting, that so captivates him?

"The dahlia responds to nurture, and you can grow them large and impressive, but you've got to disbud and disbranch, fertilize rightly, and water rightly. It's kind of a temperamental flower," the professor told me. "And a person is not always successful. But you keep trying.

"A person falls in love with nature, with plants, with the process of growing and seeing things go from seed to flower," Hein said as a lone incandescent blue dragonfly buzzed our heads. "It teaches you something about life. It not only soothes the spirit; it brings a sense of peace and satisfaction. It's kind of hard to put into words. It's medicine for the spirit."

Soothes the soul. Calms the mind. And heralds the holy.

Oh, Henry, thank you.

> Lord, the air smells good today,
> straight from the mysteries
> within the inner courts of God.
> A grace like new clothes thrown
> across the garden, free medicine for everybody.
> The trees in their prayer, the birds in praise,
> the first blue violets kneeling.
> Whatever came from Being is caught up in being, drunkenly
> forgetting the way back.

—Rumi

Some People Are Like Chickens 12

In Tanzania, things went badly with Phil right from the start. It didn't help that when we first met the man who would be taking us on safari to the Ngorongoro Crater for several days, it was unexpected and unannounced, poolside at the Impala Hotel.

I can say unequivocally that I never, ever want to meet anyone for the first time while I'm wearing a bathing suit. To be more specific, I would rather have my teeth cleaned by a obsessive-compulsive dentist (off his meds) than be introduced to someone while I'm sporting a one-piece granny suit with four days worth of growth on my legs (not to mention under my arms) and a terrible case of the trots.

But that is precisely the nightmarish scene that unfolded for me when Phil and another fellow from the travel agency who had arranged the Tanzania portion of our trip ambushed us while my husband, Maurice, and I were power napping in a couple of secluded chaises by the pool. We had just endured that morning a harrowing six-hour minibus ride from Nairobi to Arusha on what was called, ironically, "The Impala Shuttle." (Impalas are far more graceful.) We were attempting to recover with a little shut-eye and a dose of vitamin-D sunshine when I heard an unfamiliar man's voice.

"You have a girl's name."

That was Phil's opening line. To my husband.

Squinting into the sun while attempting nonchalantly to throw a towel over my hirsute self, I looked up and tried to focus on Phil's face, sure that he was kidding.

He wasn't.

"When I saw your name on the tickets I thought, *Moe-reese*, that's not a man's name; that's the name for a *lay-deeee*—ha ha ha ha ha," Phil (not his real name) elaborated.

Maury laughed his most convincing fake laugh, not wanting to be misconstrued as a (dreaded) ugly American. This must be a cultural thing, we thought. Best to go along with it. So we giggled and smiled and listened to Phil make fun of my husband's Christian name for a few more minutes before he told us what time he'd be picking us up in the morning—and then ordered us to get some sleep.

"You cannot go to Ngorongoro in this condition," Phil said before stomping away toward the open-air lobby.

The next day, Phil arrived at the Impala to collect us with

a handful of airline tickets for the ensuing leg of our nearly monthlong African journey. They were mostly wrong. No ticket to Zanzibar; the wrong days and times for our Malawi flights; the wrong Tanzanian city for departure on our trip home; and on at least half the tickets my surname was spelled "Farsaji." We're in Africa, not Chicago, we reminded ourselves, taking a few deep breaths, explaining the problems, smiling, and saying "Asante sana" — "Thank you very much" in Swahili. I must have *asante sana*-ed Phil 10,000 times in the days that were to follow. Not once did he offer the common response, "Karibu" — "You're welcome."

Instead Phil grunted, snatched the tickets from Maury, and said he'd take care of it, motioning for us to follow him to the parking lot where the safari vehicle — an avocado-green Land Cruiser — awaited. "You take the front seat," he told Maury, ignoring my presence entirely. He did not open the back passenger door, offer to help me in, or caution me to be careful not to hit my head — as all the other guides we'd been with in Kenya had done, even when I asked them not to fuss over me. Phil didn't wait for me to put my seat belt on before jerking the Land Cruiser into traffic and launching me into the armrest as I wrestled with the nonfunctioning safety belt, thereby inflicting the first of many bruises I'd collect on my legs, arms, and hips, courtesy of our Tanzanian tour guide.

When you find yourself a guest in a foreign land with no vehicle of your own and very little of the native tongue in your vocabulary, you rely, not unlike Blanche DuBois, on the kindness of strangers. We were at Phil's mercy. He had the car, the tickets, the money, and the map. The trip to Ngorongoro, an enormous world-renowned collapsed volcano, or caldera, with an unparalleled range of wildlife, was to last three days. It was meant to be a highlight of our African visit, and we couldn't go alone or by foot. (There are actual lions.) We had to be friends with Phil. So we made happy chitchat.

Where was he from?

"Tanzania."

Where in Tanzania?

"Here."

How long had he been a guide?

"Ten years."

Does he enjoy guiding?

"Yeah."

Hey, what's the name of that amazing tree with the red flowers?

"Dunno."

How far is it to Ngorongoro?

"Not far."

Mmm-kay. So much for the witty repartee. (For the record, it was about three hours from Arusha to Ngorongoro.)

Maury tried again, this time with a question a little more obscure. Adjacent to the Impala Hotel there is a large traffic circle. The day before, we had heard what sounded like a marching band playing on the other side of the tall hedge that surrounded the hotel grounds. My husband, as he is wont to do, went to investigate, reporting back that it appeared to be a wedding party, with a band leading the way around the roundabout, having their pictures taken. We asked a friend who lives in Arusha about it, and she said it was one of the most popular places in the Tanzanian city for wedding photo shoots. Maury asked Phil what he knew about it.

This seemed to perk up our otherwise surly guide. He told us that it is considered good luck for the bride to walk around the

traffic circle three times and then join her new husband —
something about symbolizing always returning to him no matter
where life takes her. The roundabout story reminded Phil of
another story from his childhood.

Please go on, we encouraged. Well, apparently when Phil's
grandmother would slaughter a chicken, she would always turn the
decapitated bird's corpse around a bowl three times to ward off bad
juju.

"Some people are like chickens," Phil said.

Uh-huh.

Maury and I nodded in the affirmative and said that, yes,
indeed, some people were like chickens. My husband shot me a
wary look. Phil kept driving.

We bounced along the road to Ngorongoro for long stretches
in silence, which was fine by me. The vistas we passed while
traveling west and then north were staggeringly beautiful. The
austere splendor of the lower Great Rift Valley with its moonscape-
muted colors set a striking backdrop for the dark, lanky figures
swathed in red and purple cloth we'd see walking regally while
herding cattle or simply walking in what felt to us like the middle of
nowhere. They were Maasai, the nomadic tribe that inhabits parts
of southern Kenya and northern Tanzania.

"I think the Maasai women are the most strikingly beautiful
women I've ever seen in my life," I said aloud, to no one in
particular.

"They aren't Maasai; those are Arusha people!" Phil corrected
me from the front seat.

"Oh, sorry," I said. "They look like Maasai."

"No! Arusha!"

Fast-forward three minutes. On the right side of the road, a huge open-air market is in full swing. There are women selling every kind of produce imaginable; men haggling over livestock; children playing around a few scraggly trees. There must have been a couple thousand people there, all dressed in red and purple, with elaborately beaded earrings, necklaces and armbands — precisely the kind of folks depicted in practically every photograph of a member of the Maasai tribe I'd ever seen in *National Geographic*.

"That is a Maasai market," Phil announced.

"So they are Maasai, not Arusha?" I inquired.

"No! Maasai, not Arusha!" he said with an inflection that conveyed his utter disdain for my wearisome idiocy.

If I'm not mistaken, the Maasai question I asked was the last one that Phil answered voluntarily. From time to time, I'd lob a question from the backseat about roadside attractions — "Is that a giraffe?" for instance — but my entreaty would invariably be greeted by Phil's stony silence. That is, unless my husband repeated the question, in which case we'd both receive an answer (or rather, he'd get an answer and I'd eavesdrop). Occasionally, the answers were polysyllabic, even — intelligent, educated, interesting replies from a seasoned guide who knew his stuff.

When Phil did speak to me, it was usually to make a joke at my expense: if I didn't know the name of something, when I said we didn't have time to go to the Serengeti on this visit, when Maury's Swahili was better than mine. At one point he joked that I should get out of the truck first if we see any lions to check on whether they're hungry or not. That really cracked Phil up. He laughed his butt off. No one else in the truck was laughing. Phil didn't seem to notice.

About forty-five minutes before we made our bone-jangling ascent to the Ngorongoro Game Lodge on a dirt "road" of narrow switchbacks and potholes so big they could swallow my old Miata whole, Phil announced he was stopping for water and pulled into the parking lot of a tiny shop along the side of the road. He got out of the car without looking back, and Maury followed to get water for both of us, leaving me alone in the truck. It was about 90 degrees outside, but I kept the windows shut (as previously cautioned by our guide in Kenya) because I saw them coming. The hawkers. A half dozen of them—old women and young men—shaking their wares at the window and asking me to make a purchase.

One particularly brazen teenager pried the window next to me open and asked where I was from. (By the way, if you are an American and ever find yourself in similar circumstances, the answer is always "Canada"—stumps them every time.) But I said Chicago, and all bets were off. A toothless crone shoved beaded necklaces in my face, and the pushy kid told me I wanted a T-shirt that said, "Only elephants should wear ivory."

"It's a good shirt, good expression," he said—and I agreed with him.

When I said I didn't have any money—and I really didn't have a single shilling on me—the kid asked if I had anything to barter. Shoving my laptop deeper under my seat with one foot, and my camera bag farther away from the window with my hip, the first thing I found when I put my hand in my purse was a bottle of 45 SPF sunscreen, which he grabbed from me.

Tossing the elephant T-shirt through the open window, he said dubiously, "This is for sunburn."

"I know," I said, "but it's really all I have."

"How about 10,000 shillings?" he asked.

"I don't have anything. My husband does. He's inside," I said, pointing toward the shop.

Just then, Maury and Phil returned to the truck after what had been about a minute but felt like an eternity. A small, increasingly rowdy crowd had gathered outside my window. I asked Maury for 10,000 shillings (about 10 bucks), which he gave me without question, and handed it to the teenager before Phil began yelling in Swahili.

He shooed the crowd and pulled away, then reeled around in his seat and said to me, "If you want to buy something, you ask me! You should have had two T-shirts for 10 dollars — THREE in Arusha! He was a thief. You ask me first!"

Now . . . let it be known that, while I consider myself a feminist, I am not the kind of woman who easily gets her knickers in a twist over a man's choice of words, tone of voice, or passing condescension. Being ridiculed and bullied by the guy being well paid to drive us from one place to another was an entirely different universe. It was the culmination of a day of effrontery, and I'd had enough of his officious thuggishness. It was like being on safari with 50 Cent.

So I did the mature thing and gave Phil the silent treatment and Maury the stink eye until we reached the lodge.

A word about my husband, lest anyone get the impression that his chivalry is somehow lacking: Maury is the quintessential pro-feminist man, a cross between Alan Alda and Al Franken. He lets me take care of myself, but if called upon, he could fly tackle a guy and put him in a wrestler's hold, like Franken did to that aggressive heckler at a Howard Dean stump speech in New Hampshire during the 2004 presidential campaign. Had Phil crossed the line into threatening territory, Maury would have been on him like an Irish prizefighter. But until I gave him the distress signal, my husband let me fend for myself, though he, too, was less than pleased with our guide's gruff demeanor and obvious issues with women.

Dithering with rage, when we arrived at Ngorongoro a short while later, I couldn't even see the crater. Blinded by my anger, I plunked myself down in an incongruous-if-cozy Adirondack chair at sunset on the lanai at the edge of one of the world's most extraordinary natural wonders. But looking down into the vast, ethereal green-gray landscape, the only thing I could see was a void and my enmity. I was livid with Phil for ruining that moment for me, for making me wish the people next to me, who were squealing with delight about spotting the silhouette of an elephant in their binoculars, would just pipe down so I could concentrate on being pissed off. Maury tried to ply me with a rum and diet Coke. It didn't help. And then Fiddy reappeared, offering to get us both a cup of coffee or tea. I ignored him.

Instead, as soon as our keys turned up, I stormed off to the room, full of venom and righteous indignation. I slammed suitcases around while Maury calmly drew open the curtains to expose a view of the caldera as good if not better than the one from the terrace above us. I still couldn't see it.

After I finished washing my face and setting out toiletries for the morning, I opened the bathroom door where my husband greeted me, smiling like a right doofus.

"Guess who our room steward is?" he chirped.

"What?" I snapped.

"Our *room steward*—guess who this sign says our *room steward* is?" he said, grinning and bouncing a little from foot to foot.

"WHAT?!" I said, glaring at him.

Then Maury held up a small plastic plaque that read, "Your room steward is ... " in white letters on a worn green background, and the name "GRACE" written in bold black letters underneath.

Grace. OK. Duly noted.

I don't need a burning bush or pillar of fire.

God's little "lighten up, Francis" plastic memo made me burst out laughing at my own ridiculousness, at the comedy of the whole experience. Maury and I ended up having a marvelous, romantic, candlelit, Phil-free evening on the edge of the wild (which I could finally see.) It was delightful, just as I imagined it would be.

The next morning, we were on time (early, even) to meet Phil and were the first Land Rover out of the gate and into the park. Off to a fresh start, looking for lions and hippos and all manner of wildlife not normally encountered in the Midwest.

A couple of weeks before our visit to Ngorongoro, we had gone on a two-day game drive at Lake Nakuru in Kenya with two traveling companions—our guides, Sammy and Simon—whom we adored. In Kenya we encountered nearly every kind of animal the word *safari* conjures in the mind. Zebras so plentiful and ubiquitous we began referring to them as "squirrels." Hundreds of water buffalo. Giraffes. White rhinos. Warthogs. Thomson's gazelles. Green vervet monkeys and curious colobus monkeys with their long black-and-white manes. Troop after troop of baboons. And two male lions dozing on a shady rock outcropping about twenty feet above our heads. It was a magical couple of days full of zoological fireworks.

But there were no elephants at Lake Nakuru. That was one of the many reasons for our trip to Ngorongoro. If Phil's information was correct, about eighty older bachelor elephants with long tusks live in the park, and if we got lucky, we might see three or four during our drive. The prospect made me giddy. I love elephants. So it was with great anticipation and optimism that I climbed back into Phil's truck in the predawn chill — bygones gone — ready for the adventure of a lifetime.

Our sunny disposition lasted about ten minutes. The optimism bubble burst the second time Phil told one or the other of us to "hurry up" while we were trying to take a photograph. About an hour into the daylong drive, after he had tossed us both around the back of the Land Rover with his too-fast-for-the-terrain driving, not stopping when we politely asked him to so we could get a better look at a massive herd of wildebeests and making a few more jokes about feeding me to various wild things, a pall had settled over the truck. I gave up and sat down in the middle of the backseat and just stared out the window instead of standing up, head and shoulders exposed in the open safari pop-up.

Maury tried to make the best of it, but after a while, he sat down too. There we were in the middle of a glorious natural wonder, trying to drink it in while whizzing through it like we were late for an appointment. When Phil did stop the truck to show us something, invariably it was a tiny something a half-mile away, and when we couldn't immediately pick it out — he gave helpful instructions such as "over there" and "right there," while pointing into the vast sweep of the caldera — he'd get frustrated and begin to pull away unless we pleaded with him to stop and promised to do our best to see what he was trying to show us. Sometimes

I just faked it. It seemed to be the path of least resistance on our increasingly codependent safari.

By the time we stopped for lunch, I was fuming again, admiring a fresh hematoma the size and color of a ripe plum on the back of my left thigh and sputtering expletives under my breath. When Phil exited the Land Rover to take his lunch outside, Maury and I discussed our displeasure at the predicament and our resignation to just get through it as quickly as possible and get back to the lodge for dinner. I let loose a diatribe of angst and fury about how unprofessional Phil was and how he'd spoiled the trip and how we should word our complaint to the main office when we returned to Arusha. Only after Maury made a trip to the men's room did we realize Phil had been sitting on the truck's bumper the whole time.

"I don't think he heard it," Maury said. "He doesn't hear anything. He doesn't listen."

"But what if he did?" I moaned. "Well, maybe he needed to hear it."

When Phil climbed back into the truck for what would be the last stretch of the game drive, we both smiled and tried to be gracious. If he had overheard our conversation, he didn't let on. Instead, we drove away in silence and in the opposite direction of where most of the other safari trucks were headed. We seemed to be proceeding to a more deserted part of the caldera with not much to see in the manner of animal life. Nervous homicidal visions danced in my head as the truck bounced alone into the great beyond.

That was when it occurred to me to pray. Not a please-Lord-don't-let-him-kill-us-and-leave-us-for-the-hyenas kind of prayer. Instead I started thinking about grace, which was, ostensibly, the real reason we were in Africa in the first place. We were on safari, looking for grace in the wild. I realized I had not been truly gracious to Phil. Maybe he was having a really bad day. Perhaps there were painful things going on in his life that were the root of his unpleasantness, that it had nothing to do with us, that he was unaware of his own demeanor. As God and I had a chat in the dusty backseat of the Land Rover, it became clear to me that I was so worried about missing out on grace moments with the animals that I was missing out on being a grace moment for Phil—or for Maury, for that matter. I told God I was sorry and asked God to help me be a better vessel, get out of my own way, and be present for Phil in whatever way he needed me to be.

The truck lurched to the left as Phil swung it around a fallen tree and onto a smaller path that led into a stand of trees. He slowed down almost to a stop.

"There," he said.

Maury and I stood up in the truck's open safari top and looked toward the spot where Phil was pointing. In a clearing about 100 yards away was an elephant with long, curved tusks, pulling at the leaves of a tree with its trunk.

It was about the most beautiful thing I've ever seen. We were close enough to hear the pachyderm's snuffling and the crack of the branches as it pulled them into its mouth. We must have stayed there for ten minutes, stock-still but for the fluttering of the camera shutter, staring in awe at the splendid creature. Phil asked us if he should pull ahead, and we said, "Yes, thank you," that we could go home happy now that we'd seen an elephant, that our safari work was done. For a split second, I thought I caught the hint of a smile on our guide's face, but it might have been my (ever fertile) imagination.

Phil pulled forward a few hundred yards and stopped again. "Look," he said, "over there."

There were two more elephants, one larger than the other, throwing dirt onto their backs with their trunks. A bath, Phil explained. These two were even closer than the first one had been. We watched again in awe for many minutes, cooing like contented babies while capturing it all on film. Then Phil drove on.

We thanked him profusely for finding the elephants, saying that it indeed had been a highlight of our African visit, and asking again what he knew about the park's elephants. He shared a bit more of what he knew — how these were older elephants that lived in the caldera because they'd been chased off by the younger bulls in herds just outside the park who wanted the female elephants all to themselves. Occasionally the old fellas would wander out to the herd, and the young bulls would chase them back into the caldera. The way he described them led me to think of the two we'd just seen as the archetypal middle-aged bachelors, Oscar Madison and Felix Unger of *The Odd Couple*.

We stopped to use the bathroom at the last outpost in the caldera before making our ascent back to the lodge. For a few minutes, I was alone with Phil.

"We are at the end of the circuit," he said. "Do you want to see more or should we return to the lodge?"

"I think we're good. It's been a long day, and those elephants were just amazing."

"OK, then. We'll head back," Phil said.

As we turned to drive out of the caldera, there it was — another elephant. A big one. The largest we'd seen, standing in the field behind the rest stop.

Magnificent. Totally unexpected. A bonus elephant.

"OK, God," I thought, "now you're just showing off."

For reasons I cannot explain
There's some part of me wants to see Graceland

—Paul Simon

Aluminum Mary 13

This is a love story.

An unlikely love story, perhaps, but a true love story just the same.

Not ten minutes after meeting her for the first time in the shadow of a thirty-three-foot-tall metallic statue of the Virgin Mary at a convent in the Rust Belt suburbs of Chicago's south side, Sister Annunziata told me she loved me.

Reaching out an elegant, wizened hand from her wheelchair to touch my cheek, she first asked me whether I was Irish and then said, "You have the face of an angel."

I was a goner.

Annunziata, who was eighty-three at the time, had me completely from that moment forward — utterly devoted to her for the rest of her life. I was Annunziata's and she was mine — and that was that. She became the Maude to my Harold, showing me how to love without limits.

Falling helplessly in love with an octogenarian wheelchair-bound Roman Catholic nun was not exactly what I had been expecting those many summers ago when I was a cub reporter dispatched to the convent in a town called Blue Island to write a story about the giant statue of the Virgin Mary (nicknamed "Aluminum Mary" by us snarky newsroom denizens). The pet project of an eccentric Catholic businessman, the statue had been drawing huge crowds as it made the rounds from parish to parish on the back of a flatbed truck.

I've never had much use for saints and their statues and never truly understood people's devotion to them, even to the Virgin. My parents had christened me with the middle name Mary, at the time a sign of my mother's religious devotion and the namesake of my godmother, my mother's only living sister, Mary. As a child, I would visit my great-aunt Sister Mary Charles, a Sister of Mercy nun, at her convent in Connecticut, and spend hours studying the statues of the young woman in blue the sisters referred to as "Our Lady" with the same kind of fascination I lavished on my dolls. The statues were like giant stone and plaster versions of the Madame Alexander dolls that my mother collected for me and that I doted on cautiously, careful to not damage their delicately fashioned limbs or muss their taffeta costumes and elaborately plaited hair.

As I set out that hot summer afternoon to see the enormous metal statue of Our Lady of the New Millennium, as it officially was called, I figured the reward would be some kitschy anecdotes about the devotees who flocked to pray at its enormous feet. When I arrived, a few dozen people—mostly pensioners and women with their young children—had gathered in folding chairs beside the flatbed truck that carried the giant Mary to recite the Rosary. There were dozens of roses and bouquets of supermarket flowers propped up at the statue's gleaming feet, dozens more tall votive candles flickering in the light breeze, handwritten petitions on scraps of paper, and prayer cards with familiar images of Our Lady of Guadalupe and the dark Lady of Czestochowa tucked here and there.

As I strolled across the courtyard of Our Lady of Sorrows convent, a clutch of older ladies wearing badges identifying them as members of the Blue Army—die-hard Marian devotees—greeted me as I approached the assembled crowd and invited me to join them in a decade or two of the Rosary and bring my own concerns to the Virgin in prayer. I thanked them but declined, explaining that I was a journalist and was only there to observe, not participate.

I found a chair off to the side and watched as the group prayed in English, Spanish, Polish, and Italian, marveling at the devotion I couldn't quite fathom. Some of the penitents knelt in the lush grass or on the pavement. A few stood alone, quietly weeping. After watching for an hour or so, I dutifully approached a number of people and asked why they'd come to see the statue, what the experience meant to them, what they were hoping to accomplish or feel, spiritually or otherwise. They told me about illnesses and lost souls, about how the Virgin Mary had drawn near to them in prayer, how she loved all people and was the last great hope for a world gone mad. I wrote down their names and their stories and moved back to my seat to reflect on what they'd said and to bask in the amber light and encroaching cool of the evening.

It was about this time that something caught my attention out of the corner of my eye. I turned to see an elderly nun sitting in a wheelchair in the shade, a thick black cardigan pulled tightly around her hips. She was looking at me and was waving, beckoning me to her.

Her name was Annunziata, she told me, grabbing my hands and pulling me low to her. I crouched down and introduced myself, and that's when she said I had the face of an angel.

"She's our mother," Sister Annunziata said of the massive statute looming in the distance. "She's everyone's mother. I don't know what I'd do without her."

I stayed there for a while, holding hands with this elderly nun, who was a stranger to me but who felt like family.

As I stood to leave, explaining that I had to return to the newspaper and write my story, Annunziata asked if I'd come visit her again. I said I would.

"I love you," she said.

"I love you too," I found myself saying. And I meant it.

Why do so many people have such a hard time saying, "I love you"? They ration those words, as if their meaning could be somehow cheapened or diminished were they said too many times to too many people. Is it possible to love too much? Too recklessly? Unconditionally and indiscriminately?

No. There is nothing better in life than knowing you are loved. There is no more precious gift, no sweeter burden.

A few weeks later, I returned to Our Lady of Sorrows to see Annunziata. She was waiting for me in the convent's first-floor dayroom in her wheelchair, smiling and spreading her arms wide as if I were her long-lost child. She had tears in her eyes, and the first thing she said was, "Oh, I love you so much!" Then she giggled. She was always giggling, a bubbling stream of joyful laughter that made her seem more like a silly schoolgirl than a wise, holy woman.

She wanted to know all about me, about my family, my mother and father, Sister Mary Charles, where I grew up, what I studied, what I liked to read, how I fell in love with my husband, whether I hoped to have children someday, why I had become a writer. I told her my stories with no holds barred. She was my instant confessor and listened to my stories as if they were the most riveting she'd ever heard.

Annunziata told me her stories too. How she'd entered the Mantellate Sisters Servants of Mary religious order in 1937, when she was twenty-one years old. That she was the child of Sicilian immigrants and grew up in an Italian neighborhood in Chicago that had been transformed into something she didn't recognize with high-rise public housing and violent crime. She told me she disliked her given name, Biaggia, and hated the Americanized nickname "Bessie," bestowed on her in grade school; that she couldn't wait to get her religious name, Annunziata; and that her sister, Marie, had been the pretty one. When I said she was beautiful—and she really was—she got cross with me and said she had a fat face, that she'd never been pretty. I told her she was ridiculous, and we agreed to disagree.

Over the years, in subsequent visits, which were never as often as I would have liked them to be, Annunziata told me stories about her students in Blue Island and in Rome, where she lived and taught from 1958 to 1972. She was an English teacher, a voracious reader, a true lover of language, art, and film. One afternoon, she revealed that her favorite film was *Casablanca*.

"Not *The Bells of Saint Mary's* or *The Song of Bernadette*?" I said jokingly.

"Oh, no. I looooooooove *Casablanca*! It's so romantic, such a sad love story," she swooned.

At the time we were in the small room in the convent's infirmary where she'd been moved some months earlier as her health began to fail. She was unhappy there and missed being on the ground floor where she could see the visitors who came to call on the other sisters, where it had been her job to answer the main phone line, a responsibility she loved because she got to talk to all sorts of people. In the infirmary she felt isolated and old.

As she talked about her years in Rome and more about *Casablanca*, Annunziata fished out a stack of photos from the bureau next to the easy chair where she slept because it was more comfortable for her than the single bed. She handed me a small black-and-white snapshot of a much younger Annunziata standing with two uniformed Catholic schoolgirls. "Those were her daughters," she said.

"Whose daughters?" I asked.

The pretty Swedish actress, she said, the one whose name was escaping her. I looked closer, and one of the girl's faces looked familiar. I couldn't place it at first, and then she said, "Ilsa." The Catholic schoolgirl in the photograph, the one smiling shyly next to a beaming younger Annunziata was Ingrid Bergman's daughter, Isabella Rossellini. I said the names — Bergman, Rossellini — and the nun's face lit up. "Oh, yes! Yes, that's her!"

"They were so cruel to her; they said such awful things," she said of Bergman. "I felt so sorry for her. She had these beautiful daughters. I couldn't understand why people were so cruel to her." Annunziata was talking about the controversy that had swirled around Ingrid Bergman nearly a half century before, when the Swedish actress (who, of course, played the role of Ilsa in *Casablanca*), a married mother of one, had a love affair with the Italian director Roberto Rossellini, became pregnant, and gave birth to his son in 1950. It was absolutely scandalous at the time, and Bergman became something of a pariah. She even was denounced on the floor of the United States Senate as "a horrible example of womanhood and a powerful influence for evil" and was, by a floor vote, officially declared persona non grata in the United States. Bergman, who lived in self-imposed exile in Italy, divorced from her first husband, married Rossellini and in 1952 gave birth to twin daughters, Isabella and Isotta, who were, for a time, Annunziata's students in Rome. At least that's the story she told each time she brought out the photograph. Though I couldn't be sure, I chose to believe her.

The way Bergman was treated by the church, by the establishment, by the so-called keeper of society's moral authority, haunted Annunziata, this pious woman who loved everyone with abandon. It pained her, troubling her soul into her last days on earth. She was so sensitive to cruelty, judgmentalism, the absence of forgiveness and grace even or perhaps especially when it came to those she didn't know. It's one of the greatest lessons she taught me, and she taught me so very much.

In the last year of her life, Annunziata was sick much of the time. She wanted to die, she said, to "go home" to Jesus, her Lord, her love, her "bride." Each time I talked to her, she'd ask me to pray for her to die in her sleep. She wasn't afraid of death, but she didn't want to suffer. Her body, she said, was falling apart. She was frustrated and scared. "Everything is just so icky," she told me one day as a dark mood flashed across her otherwise cherubic face when she couldn't recall what she'd been talking about moments earlier. "I used to read profusely. To tell me I can't read anymore is so mean to me," she said, clenching her birdlike hand into a fist around the gold crucifix ring with a half-inch of yarn wound around the band to hold it in place. "Sometimes I stand up and I feel so bad, like I'm going to die. I get so angry because I want to be going on my way, but I keep pulling back through."

She thought for a few moments and then the familiar smile returned to her face. "The end is near. It's soon. I know it is. I'm not afraid. Not at all. God is so good," she said. "I'm going to die while I'm sleeping. I'm depending on you for that." I told her I'd pray for that, and I did.

On one of our last visits a few months before she went home to her bride, I brought a copy of *Casablanca* and we watched it together on an old television set the size of a steamer trunk in the infirmary's lounge. We didn't say much during the movie, except to comment on how beautiful Ingrid Bergman was. Mostly we sat in rapt silence next to each other, sipping superstrong, supersweet espresso coffee in tiny porcelain cups one of the Italian sisters brought up from the kitchen downstairs.

After the movie, a nurse and I helped Annunziata back to her room a few feet away. As I said good-bye to her in the shadowy room and tucked her into her easy chair with an afghan, she grabbed my hand and pulled me close to her face as she often did. "I love you so much," she said.

Those were the last words she ever spoke to me.

Sister Annunziata died in her sleep on July 22, 2002. She was eighty-six. At her funeral a few days later in the chapel at Our Lady of Sorrows, the priest presiding at the Mass mentioned her smile. It was a sign of her hospitality, he said, which was a central part of her vocation as a servant of the Virgin Mary.

My nun, which is how I think of her, was the most profound witness for God's love I've ever encountered in this world. She was a magnet for lost souls, a petite fortress of strength and unconditional love. What this sprightly, silly, lovely woman did from the obscurity of a faded convent in Rust Belt Chicago was to fulfill in a passionate, tireless way the supreme commandment of Jesus' gospel every day of her life. According to the thirteenth chapter of the gospel of John in the New Testament, just after Jesus washed the feet of his twelve disciples (including the one he knew would betray him and deliver him into the hands of his executioners), he gave them an order: "Love one another. As I have loved you, so you must love one another. By this everyone will know that you are my disciples, if you love one another."

When Annunziata said she loved me or any of her thousands of other friends and beloveds, she was really saying, at least in my mind, "God loves you." To quote the singer/songwriter James

Taylor, she showered the people she loved with love, always showing the way that she felt without holding back.

Even as her body could barely contain her soul any longer, she'd open wide the gates of herself with a smile, that giggle, her twinkling eyes, and she'd let the supernatural love flow through her.

Walking out of the chapel after her funeral, a woman I'd never seen before stopped me and said, "You're Cathleen, aren't you?"

"Yes," I croaked, tears rolling off my nose as I fingered the prayer card with Annunziata's picture on it.

Slipping an arm around my shoulders, the woman explained that she was one of Annunziata's former students and said, "She loved you so much."

I know.

Our choice is this. It is to choose to believe that the truth of our story is contained in Jesus' story, which is a love story. Jesus' story is the truth about who we are and who the God is who Jesus says loves us. It is the truth about where we are going and how we are going to get there, if we get there at all, and what we are going to find if we finally do. Only for once let us not betray the richness and depth and mystery of that truth by trying to explain it.

—Frederick Buechner

Wet Skunk

14

A writer.

One who writes.

Sometimes writers are people who make their living writing things — things like newspaper articles, short stories, greeting cards, or books.

I am a writer, supposedly, in that I earn my wages writing. I also consider it my vocation, in the spiritual sense of that word. I feel called to write. By God. (No pressure.)

So when the words don't come, when I am "blocked," as various psychoanalysts and writing coaches refer to the phenomenon, a certain sense of dread begins to creep in like the smell of skunk through the car vents.

There are a number of options for dealing with a sudden, all-consuming, nearly paralytic attack of what I prefer to call "the skunks." I can hold my breath until the overwhelming stench is gone and I'm able to breathe fresh air again. I can rejig the ventilation system — turn the air-conditioning on and off, open the windows, close the windows, blast the fan, re-aim the vents — and drive faster, trying to outrun it. Or I can inhale the choking stink in big gulps until, like an overzealous application of perfume, I can no longer smell it.

For one miserable, muggy stretch of a recent late July and early August, the skunks came for what, in the throes of trying to get rid of them, began to feel like a permanent visit. I tried everything to shake them. I read. I walked. I prayed. I tried to listen for God's voice. I meditated and listened to Tibetan gong music. I slept. I cooked. I ate — boy, did I eat. I drank wine. I didn't drink wine. I drank coffee. I didn't drink coffee. I turned the phones off and banned myself from email — all four accounts.

I tried working at night (when there's less competition for the good ideas, as an author friend once told me). I tried working early in the morning, in the middle of the afternoon; in bed; in the backyard under my mulberry tree, Henry; at the public library; and in the local coffeehouse where stay-at-home moms go to sip lattes and let their kids mingle freely for a few minutes while they indulge in adult camaraderie with sister sojourners.

Still, nothing was happening. I had all these wonderful ideas, images, experiences, conversations, turns of phrase, but when I sat down in front of the blank page—or empty computer screen, in my case—nothing. Bupkes. Nada. *Rien.*

Only sheer panic.

In the midst of this siege of the skunks, a friend, who had given birth to her second child not too long before, told me that there's a period during pregnancy where many women feel like they may never actually have the baby—like they may be pregnant forever. It's an irrational fear, of course, but no less terrifying when you're nine months pregnant and counting.

What she meant, of course, is that I wouldn't have the skunks forever. I was pregnant with ideas, and I would give birth when it was time—and no amount of pushing, walking, holding my breath, changing the ventilation, venue, or menu was going to make the delivery come any sooner.

I had to let go, she said. Unfortunately, that's not my strong suit. I'd rather smell the skunk and worry about measuring the effectiveness of tomato juice baths versus dangerously heavy doses of Febreze. (Neither works well, by the way. You only end up smelling like a tomato- or "mountain breeze"-flavored skunk.)

One particularly skunky Wednesday in August, after not having left the house for two days—and not having written a word of anything approaching artful—I decided to walk to the local stationery store to buy birthday cards for my father, and then to the coffee shop for a pound of mocha java (even though I wasn't actually drinking it at the time).

No makeup, sleep in my eyes, and my hair in a messy bun, I threw on a pair of cutoff shorts, flip-flops, one of a dozen black tank tops in a pile on the closet floor, and (for once) a bra; grabbed my sunglasses and purse and headed out the door. It was overcast and humid, but that's pretty much what summer is in Chicago much of the time. Rain could fall at any moment, but usually all we get is muggy.

So without a second thought about truly inclement weather, I sallied forth on my meager errands, hoping the walk would do me some psychological good, or at the very least burn a few of the calories I'd been hoarding like a neurotic squirrel before the first snowfall.

The card shop is about four blocks away, and by the time I'd walked there and picked out three cards—a serious one from me, a funny one from my husband, and one from the grandcats—it had started to sprinkle. When I arrived at the coffee shop two blocks farther away, the weather had turned into a Midwestern monsoon. After paying for my pound of coffee, I stood around for a few minutes while the shop started to get crowded with wet, grumbling customers. I text-messaged a couple of friends, looked around for a seat and a paper I hadn't already read (there weren't any), and decided to abandon ship.

I ran a couple of doors down to the Pier 1 store and wandered for a while, looking at various throw pillows and scented candles I vaguely wanted but didn't need, waiting for the downpour to relent. But it didn't. It kept coming—harder, faster, in big cartoonish drippy-drops. I thought about ducking into the bookstore across the street and lingering there until the storm passed, but it was a *book*store. I might as well have run back to the coffee shop and slammed double espressos until my heart exploded.

People outside were huddled in doorways like lunch-hour refugees, their faces tense from the one-two punch of getting their hair wet and being late getting back to the office. But I wasn't all dressed up and had nowhere in particular to be, so I walked out into the rain.

I didn't run. I just walked. Within a minute I was soaked—not damp or wet, but totally waterlogged. It dripped off my nose and earlobes and into my eyes so that I had to wipe water away to navigate the nearly deserted sidewalks. My shirt was drenched, and the old jean shorts I was wearing had turned from faded baby blue back to indigo. Catching a glimpse of myself in a jewelry store window, I looked as if I had just crawled out of a swimming pool.

At first, I thought people were staring. In fairness, some of them were. I wasn't darting from corner to corner with an umbrella or newspaper over my head like most everyone else. I was just walking. A wet, skunked-up writer, strolling blissfully in the downpour with a pound of coffee under my arm and a goofy smile on my face.

As I walked, I recalled a favorite experience from my college years. It happened just before the end of term my junior year, in the midst of final exams, when everyone is a little loopy from too much caffeine, not enough sleep, and cabin fever. Armed with water balloons, a bunch of girlfriends and I piled into a car and drove around like banshees chasing (and being chased) by a carload of boys carrying Super Soaker water guns and an impressive cache of water balloons. This went on for hours, much to the dismay of the campus police, who also gave chase, capturing the boys for a half-hour while we went to reload. It was a giddy, flirty night of pure, hormone-fueled fun.

Around midnight, when we'd run out of water balloons and energy, it started to pour. We got out of the car and danced in the rain, laughing and singing Indigo Girls songs into the early morning hours. When people say that college is the best time of your life, this is what they're talking about. The memory made me laugh out loud—at myself and my usual self-consciousness. How silly to worry about what I looked like or what anyone else thought. I was baptized by the rain, washed clean of ego and fret.

As I turned the corner onto the block where I live, I was skipping and splashing in puddles like a child. It reminded me of that episode of *Friends* where Rachel is embarrassed to run in the park with Phoebe because Phoebe runs wildly, arms flailing like a five-year-old hopped-up on cotton candy. When Rachel admits she doesn't want to jog with Phoebe because she is worried about what other people might think, Phoebe says, "But [they're] people that you don't know and will never see again." Rachel, still fretting, replies, "Yes, but still. They're people. With *eyes*."

Phoebe doesn't understand Rachel's fear, which is really the fear of not being good enough, of making a mistake, of not doing it right. As I walked on in the unrelenting downpour, I realized that this kind of fear is precisely what had brought on the skunks. I was worried about doing it wrong, about writing something that was less than perfect.

"That's OK, Rachel," Phoebe tells her. "I'm not judging you; that's just who you are. Me, I'm more free, ya know? I run like I did when I was a kid, 'cause that's the only way it's fun. I mean, didn't you ever run so fast you thought your legs were gonna fall off? Ya know, like when you were running toward the swings or running away from Satan?"

Rachel eventually gets it, and she starts running wild. "It's amazing, Phoebs!" she says. "I feel so free and so graceful." And then she promptly runs horse-first into a New York City mounted police officer.

With this in mind, it felt perfectly acceptable to stop in the middle of the funeral home parking lot a block from my home, put the pound of coffee on the ground, and twirl in wet circles until I was a little dizzy.

I started to laugh harder. It was the first time in a long while I had laughed so hard without the joke being at someone else's expense or because I was watching something—anything—on *Comedy Central*. I laughed at myself. I laughed at the ridiculousness of hiding from the rain when it doesn't matter if I get wet. At the foolishness of trying to get it right all the time. At the fragility of my ego, so worried about being judged by eyes that aren't even there. At the joy of the moment. At the birthday cards, safe and dry in a plastic bag inside my otherwise waterlogged purse, protected, just as I am, always, by the One who brings the rain.

I walked up the front steps of my house, opened the door, and let the air-conditioned coolness flow over me. I stripped off my sopping-wet clothes, hopped in a warm shower, threw on my coziest bathrobe, crawled into bed with my laptop, and began to write.

I know nothing except what everyone knows—
If there when Grace dances, I should dance.

—W. H. Auden

Passing Over 15

My rabbi—yes, I have a rabbi—once told me that I would learn the most about myself from the people I think are the least like me. That is how I came to spend Easter, and all of Passover, traveling around Montana in an SUV with the state's only resident rabbi, his wife, and their Schnauzer.

For five years, Allen Secher was the only rabbi living full-time in Montana, a state with a population of 900,000 and a tiny Jewish community of about 1,100. Allen and his wife, Ina, reside in Whitefish, Montana, in the northwest corner of the state, but for two weeks every month, they hit the road as itinerant clergy, serving a congregation in Bozeman four hours south and traveling wherever else they are beckoned to preside at weddings, bar mitzvahs, bat mitzvahs, baby-naming ceremonies, funerals, and interfaith events where he usually is the one and only representative of the Jewish community.

I long had heard of Allen in Chicago, where he lived for many years and was something of a legend for being the only rabbi (at least for many years) who would officiate at interfaith weddings, a practice that is still very much taboo in most Jewish circles. His best friend is my favorite Catholic priest, and he is also a dear friend of Reverend Stan, my favorite clergyperson in the world. So when I was thinking about how I might look at grace from perspectives I hadn't seen it from yet and taking my very wise rabbi's advice about encountering my "opposite" as a spiritual exercise, I got a wild hair one day and phoned the Sechers to see if I might spend Passover and Easter with them in Montana, where they had moved from Chicago when Allen retired a few years earlier.

The trip was a leap of faith for all of us, since we'd never met and would be traveling together and living in close quarters for more than a week. Happily, the Sechers, who are in their seventies and way hipper than I ever could hope to be, and I quickly learned that we are kindred spirits, always game for a new adventure. Allen was one of the original Freedom Riders — civil rights activists, summoned by Dr. Martin Luther King Jr. himself, who rode buses into the segregated South and marched in the streets as a means of protesting racist bus policies — and spent more than a few days in jail for his efforts. Both Allen and Ina were among the first graduates of Brandeis University, the only Jewish-founded secular university in the United States, and long have been pioneers of one kind or another. After finishing his rabbinical studies at a Reform seminary, Allen (who had been strictly Orthodox at Brandeis) served congregations in Mexico City and California before growing disillusioned with the rabbinate itself. He left and for twenty years dabbled in radio and acting — documentary film and television (where he eventually earned seven Emmy awards) — before a group of like-minded friends in Chicago essentially drafted him back into the ministry in the early 1990s. He founded an esoteric Jewish Renewal congregation there called Makom Shalom, where congregants worshiped in the round and meditated, and where everyone was included, regardless of gender, age, and even religion. "Sech," as I came to call him, is a true vanguard, a rebel soul searching for what is real. He's the kind of person I'm drawn to, as the Irish poet Seamus Heaney says, "like well water far down."

Even as we found common ground apart, that is, from our shared natural inclination toward general insubordination, during those first few hours in the car — Allen and I both love Sinatra (he hosts a weekly Old-Blue-Eyes-only show every Sunday night on a Kalispell, Montana, radio station), Ina and I have frighteningly similar taste in books, and Farfel (the Schnauzer) could be the twin of the German terrier I had as a child — I wondered if we would be able to overcome theological differences, even with our open minds, when it came to grace.

As I understood it, there is a concept of grace in the Jewish tradition, but it differs from the theology of grace that is central to Christianity. Before I hit the road with the Sechers, I asked a couple of Jewish theologians how the Christian and Jewish ideas of grace were similar and where they diverged. Grace, they told me, only applies to sins and transgressions that are committed between God and us. When it comes to trespasses against other people, you must first gain the forgiveness of those you wronged before you may seek God's forgiveness. There is, however, a caveat, one rabbi told me. If you ask someone's forgiveness three times, and they don't forgive you, then God will forgive you anyway, and the onus transfers to the person who wouldn't forgive you.

I have a dear friend in Chicago who works for the Jewish Federation. When I write about grace in my weekly column in the *Sun-Times*, often she calls or writes to talk about it. Invariably she stumbles over the same theological speed bump. She can grasp the kind of grace I talk about until she gets to, as she says, "the Susan Smith problem." Smith is the South Carolina woman who, in October 1991, murdered her three-year-old and fourteen-month-old sons by driving her car into a lake with the boys strapped in their car seats. "Nope," my friend says. "That's where grace doesn't work for me. I can't believe that you just get to say 'I'm sorry' and God says, 'OK, you're forgiven.' I don't think grace covers that kind of sin."

As the Sechers and I drove through the middle of Montana on a brilliantly sunny spring afternoon, passing swollen streams where the sunlight danced on undulating water like a billion diamonds—like God making "jazz hands" at us, we decided— it became clear that, while we may not have the same technical understanding of grace in relation to sin, we certainly understood in the same way the grace inherent in nature. After a few days on the road, the rabbi took to pointing out circling hawks, rainbows over mountain meadows, or especially beautiful vistas and saying, "Look! Grace!" For the rest of the trip we referred to that particular spiritual practice (and car game) as "gracespotting." Eventually, the gracespotting extended past natural wonders to the effluvia of everyday living.

Finding a tub of their favorite hummus on sale at Costco? Grace.

Talking their way onto the ski lift at Whitefish Basin for a spectacular ride up the side of the mountain on Easter morning without having to pay? Grace.

Getting the very last reservation at the best steak joint in town after a long day on the road? Grace.

Watching the final season premiere of *The Sopranos*, bundled together in our jammies on their living room couch? Grace.

Farfel sneaking her way into the guest room to sleep with me the night I was feeling particularly homesick? Grace.

Together, we spotted grace all over the place, a joyful exercise that really brought us together. After a few days we weren't strangers anymore; we were family.

And that, too, was grace.

Walking into the Emerson Center for the Performing Arts in downtown Bozeman for the first of three Seders that Allen would lead and we'd attend during the eight days of Passover, the first person to greet us was a Kinky Friedman look-alike wearing a black Stetson and holding a magnum of Australian merlot. He gamely showed us to our table while Allen did a mic check, and Ina quickly put me to work distributing the *haggadot* — liturgical booklets everyone would follow along with during the meal.

Passover is about storytelling. Specifically, it's about retelling the story of how God led the Israelites out of slavery in Egypt and, eventually, into the Promised Land. The Passover haggadah takes Seder-goers through the story of the exodus, step-by-step, with accompanying prayers, songs, food—dishes that each have spiritual significance—and drink. Each table has a Seder plate that contains (traditionally) six items: *maror* (usually horseradish), symbolizing the bitterness of slavery; *charoset* (a sweet mixture, typically, of apples, honey, and nuts), meant to represent the mortar used by the Jewish slaves to build storehouses for their Egyptian masters; *karpas* (bitter herbs such as parsley) that are dipped in salt water to symbolize tears shed; *z'roa* (traditionally it's a roasted lamb shank bone) representing the Passover (Pesach) sacrifice; and the *beitzah* (a roasted, *not boiled*, egg) that also symbolizes sacrifice as well as mourning for the destruction of the temple. An egg is typically the first thing served to mourners after a funeral.

None of this was new to me. As a religion journalist I'd attended a few Seders over the years. But through my adventure with the roving rabbi wandering the wilderness of western Montana, I came to understand Passover and the exodus in a life-changing kind of way.

During that first Seder in Bozeman, the Lone Rabbi, if you will, in his rainbow-colored yarmulke, began by explaining the basic story of the exodus, with an added twist I'd never before heard. In Hebrew, the word for Egypt is *mitzrayim*, which means "the narrow place." Just as God delivered the Jews out of their "narrow place," God is waiting to lead each of us out of our narrow places, with mercy and grace.

"Where are the narrow places in your life that you need to pass out of, that you need to be delivered from?" Allen asked. I began to think, sitting there at the rabbi's table in the middle of a couple hundred Jewish strangers. What had me backed into a corner? Where did I feel trapped, enslaved? Was it, despite priding myself on having an open mind, a narrow mind that was keeping me from walking into freedom? Do my expectations of others and myself keep me stuck in a narrow, confined place? Or is it my pathological need to control things—even transcendent experiences, how I perceive the movement of the Holy, of the Spirit—that keeps me shackled in the chains of my own fear and self-consciousness?

I needed to be delivered from myself.

That realization was my Passover miracle.

I didn't need God to part the Red Sea; I just needed my narrow mind opened a crack. What more appropriate place to pass out of my narrow place than in Montana, a true "wider place," one that's called, appropriately, "Big Sky Country." As I followed along in the haggadah, we came to the part where those gathered remember God's graciousness in specific blessing in a litany called the "Dayeinu":

> Had God brought us out of Egypt and not divided the sea
>   for us . . .
>   Dayeinu!
> Had God divided the sea and not permitted us to cross
>   to dry land . . .
>   Dayeinu!
> Had God permitted us to cross the sea on dry land and not
>   sustained us for forty years in the desert . . .
>   Dayeinu!
> Had God sustained us for forty years in the desert and not fed us
>   with manna . . .
>   Dayeinu!
> Had God fed us with manna and not given us the Sabbath . . .
>   Dayeinu!

Had God led us into the land of Israel and not built for us
    the temple . . .
                    Dayeinu!
Had God built for us the temple and not sent us prophets
    of truth . . .
                    Dayeinu!
Had God sent us prophets of truth and not made us
    a holy people . . .
                    Dayeinu!

"Dayeinu," Allen explained, means "it's enough." In other words, if God had done just one of those things, it would be enough. For me, the crack in my consciousness was enough. Dayeinu, indeed!

Several days after that first Seder in Bozeman, I went with the Sechers to a Friday night Shabbat service at the synagogue. It was, for me, Good Friday, which is usually the most maudlin, contemplative day of my year. It is the day in the Christian calendar when we recall the crucifixion of Jesus Christ. It's usually the day I spend recalling what a crappy Christian I am and how I didn't deserve by any stretch of the imagination having an incarnate God sacrifice himself on the cross in my place. What I usually have a hard time remembering on Good Friday is the grace portion of the event. That Jesus died willingly as a grace for me and the rest of the world. That even if I were as perfect as a human being can be — in heart, mind, and body — still I wouldn't be able to deserve such a sacrifice. And that's the point. That's grace.

Sitting there in the synagogue for Shabbat service with about a dozen other congregants, I wasn't dwelling on my usual Good Friday badness. When it came time to read from the

Torah—handwritten scrolls containing the first five books of the Hebrew Scriptures that are kept in a special ark in every synagogue—something happened on that April night in Montana that I'd never seen or experienced before. The Torah scrolls, kept in a blue velvet cover with gold embroidery, were taken down and passed to the congregation. I'd seen men in synagogue hold the scrolls, but I'd never seen them passed this way, from person to person, like the collection basket or the little trays of wine or bread in some of the churches I'd attended over the years.

I'm not Jewish, and in that little gathering of a dozen or so people, I think everyone there knew it. Still, when the scrolls got to me, the woman next to me, without a moment's hesitation, placed them gently in my arms, like a newborn baby. I've yet to conjure up the words to describe how that moment of inclusion felt. Sacred, yes. Grace-filled, absolutely. But also ancient—tying me to a whole history of a people whom I'd never before thought of as "mine." But they are. The Sechers are. The other people at the Bozeman synagogue were. The strangers at the supermarket where we bought matzo and wine were. The people who are reading these words are. I've never felt so alive or connected, before or since. But I'm hopeful that I'll get there again, closer now in the retelling of my story.

The Torah portion that Friday night was from the biblical book of Exodus, chapter 34, which tells the story of Moses going up on the mountain to get the tablets of the Law—the Ten Commandments—from God. This was the second set, mind you. In a fit of anger brought on by the idolatry and general nastiness of the Israelites after God had given him the first set of tablets, Moses smashed them. God beckoned him to Mount Sinai, where God gave Moses a second set, which seemed to take.

"We're all great creatures of second chances," Sech told the congregation. We expend too much energy beating ourselves up for our mistakes, screwups, and shortcomings. Fixating on them can lead to "internalized oppression," the rabbi said. "Let it go!"

Deliver yourself from your narrow, sorrowful place, he said, adding that the word for "sorrow" in Hebrew also means "narrow" and that, seeing as how it was Passover, we might want to think of that spiritual self-imprisonment as something we have to "pass through."

"Bust out into freedom," he said. "You wanna be free? Work on it!"

Each time I eat sushi now and get a little too much wasabi on my piece of ebi maki, bringing tears to my eyes and that fiery rush through my sinuses, it brings me back to the Seder table in Montana and that first taste of *maror*. And my eyes water for an entirely different reason, remembering my Passover miracle, passing over, passing through the narrow places and emerging, a free woman in Big Sky.

The Dude: *Yeah, well, the Dude abides.*
The Stranger: *"The Dude abides." I don't know about you, but I take comfort in that. It's good knowin' he's out there. The Dude—takin' 'er easy for all us sinners.*

—*The Big Lebowski*

The Purple Mamas of Asembo Bay 16

The poet Maya Angelou once said of motherhood, "To describe my mother would be to write about a hurricane in its perfect power." While on a trip to Kenya, in a tiny fishing village on the shores of Lake Victoria, I met a community of hurricanes that blew me away with gale-force grace.

Millicent was waiting impatiently for us when we arrived on a Saturday morning in Asembo Bay, hands on her hips and steely eyes boring holes into our guide, who had unwittingly flubbed our arrival time in the village about twenty-five miles from the city of Kisumu and not far from where Barack Obama's Kenyan grandmother, Sarah, still lives. We were running about an hour behind schedule, and she was not having it. After a few well-placed stern words in Swahili to our cowed and apologetic Kenyan guide, Millicent turned to my husband and me with open arms and an enormous smile. "Welcome, we are so glad you are here," she said, embracing us and grasping my hand in both of hers. "*Karibu. Karibu.* Come, see the garden."

The Women's Cooperative of Asembo Bay is a group of twenty-six widows who pool their resources and care for about seventy children (many of them orphans who have lost their parents to AIDS, a scourge that has wiped out an entire generation in villages throughout Africa and much of the developing world). In an enormous garden that stretches for several acres between the edge of Millicent's compound and the lake, the women grow kale, onions, papaya, mango, tomatoes, potatoes, and a variety of other produce and homeopathic herbs that they use for both sustenance and as a source of income.

Millicent, the cooperative's tiny ringleader, led the way at a fast clip, hopping gracefully over irrigation gullies and between rows of hard, dry earth. I was wearing flip-flops, not exactly the ideal footwear for an impromptu trek through the quasi jungle, and she kept an eagle eye on me, instinctively stretching out a hand behind her to help steady me as I galumphed through the immense garden followed by a swarm of curious dragonflies that congregated around my bare ankles.

"You can still smell it," Millicent said, stopping short in her tracks and pointing to a swath of crushed vegetation a few feet in front of us.

"Smell what?" I asked, as the only odor I could detect was the earthy combination of eucalyptus trees and freshly turned soil.

"The hippo," she said. "It ate all my sweet potatoes."

Ah, yes. I hate when that happens.

The day before, Millicent explained, the offending hippopotamus had made its way from the shores of the bay a few hundred yards away to the edge of the garden where it tore the sweet potato plants out of the ground, leaving only a few half-macerated green clumps behind, the sad remnants of a crop that had been nearly ready for harvest.

"Back home, the squirrels ate all of my tomatoes," I told her, searching for common ground. She patted my hand sympathetically. We had bonded, one gardener to another.

As we trekked back, still surrounded by the cloud of iridescent dragonflies, from the garden toward the compound where Millicent and several other widows live with their children, she began asking me questions about my life in the United States. She asked whether I had children, and when I told her that I didn't but that my husband had four grown children, Millicent looked over her shoulder at Maury, tugged me in close to her, and said in a whisper, "Oh, I didn't know that polygamy was legal in America."

After I explained that my husband had been divorced and that I am his second wife, we both crumbled into the kind of laughter that is somewhere between nervous and relieved. Maury asked what we were laughing about, and I told him I'd fill him in later.

Millicent continued to pepper me with questions about my life.

"If your husband dies, what can you do?" she asked.

"Anything you want to do," was my answer.

"Do you have to marry again, or can you live by yourself?" she pressed.

"You can live by yourself or with your children or with friends, or you can marry again—it's your choice," I said.

"*Sawa*," she said in Swahili, meaning "all right."

Then it was Millicent's turn to tell me about her life in Asembo Bay. When her husband died a number of years ago, tribal leaders in the village told her she didn't have a choice whether to marry again. She was to be given as a second wife to one of her husband's relatives. In Asembo Bay, where polygamy is practiced in some quarters and most inhabitants come from the Luo tribe, there exists a long tradition of "wife inheritance." Originally it was something of a noble concept: When a husband dies, his side of the family is responsible for the physical well-being of his widow and her children. While the widow is officially another "wife" of her brother-in-law or another male-in-law, the new relationship is meant to be nonsexual. But in recent generations, that practice changed, with the heir demanding sex from the second wife, seizing her property, and leaving her and her children destitute and, with increasing frequency, infected with the AIDS virus.

When Millicent's husband died, his relatives expected her to throw a lavish funeral feast, and if that meant selling everything she had to pay for it, so be it. She balked at their demands, and when they came to take her cow—at that point the only means of income she had—she did something radical.

"They tried to take my cow, but I said no," Millicent said, motioning to a skinny black and white heifer tethered near the grave where her husband is buried between her modest house and the chicken coop.

Millicent said no. She shirked tradition, quite literally risking her life.

No, you can't take my house.

No, you can't sell my property.

No, I won't marry him.

The community could have shunned her, or much worse. But Millicent believed she could make it on her own, with God's help. The only man she needed, she said, was Jesus.

My jaw was still on the ground when she began herding us toward a van that would take us to a neighboring compound where other members of the Women's Cooperative run a fishing business. We were just about to climb into the vehicle when Millicent spotted them — a dozen women wearing matching royal-purple dresses who emerged from a stand of trees in the distance and were moving slowly toward us in the intense late-morning heat like a procession of ancient queens.

"Ah, they got tired of waiting," Millicent said.

These were the other women from the cooperative (most of them widows ranging in age from their late teens into their early eighties), the ones who run the fishing operation about a half-mile away. We would learn later how, inspired by Millicent's quiet revolution, the Mamas, as they are known, also had rejected the practice of wife inheritance and stood up for themselves. Together, in addition to caring for dozens of children, some of whom are theirs and some orphans left behind by other villagers, the women run a number of businesses, including the farm, the fishing operation, a mill that grinds "ground nuts" (a dietary staple in this part of Kenya that are akin to peanuts and are an excellent source of protein), seven tiny shops that sell everything from steel wool to fresh eggs, and a dairy farm (with four cows).

The Mamas greeted us warmly and, after a few minutes of chiding our guide for getting us to the bay too late to watch them haul in the morning's catch and accepting his profuse apologies, they turned their attention to Maury and me and asked if we'd like to see what they do with the fish after it's brought to shore. Thirteen of us piled into the van, while others walked the distance back to the compound that houses the fishing operation. Once we arrived at the clutch of mud-and-wattle huts, Leonitta, an imposing gap-toothed woman (like the wife of Bath) we came to call "Big Mama," proudly showed us the huge nets used for fishing each morning and the ovens where the Mamas smoke the tilapia they sell to their neighbors and at a nearby market. (It's delicious.) The women had recently purchased their own boat in a revolutionary act of defiance and self-preservation. They did so because they were fed up with fishermen exploiting the young women they would send to collect the day's catch each morning. The Mamas said no to trading sex for tilapia, bought a skiff, and hired a group of young men to fish for them.

As I listened to them tell their stories, I thought of the "Proverbs woman" described in Hebrew Scripture. In chapter 31 of the biblical book of Proverbs, the ideal woman is said to rise early to provide for her family, has strong arms from all her hard work, is smart with her money and her businesses, helps neighbors in need, and wears purple garments she makes for herself. The Proverbs woman, the Bible says, is worth more than rubies. In their matching purple dresses, backs straight, heads held high, and arms finely muscled from years of manual labor, the Mamas of Asembo Bay should be valued like precious gems. Yet they have been treated as little more than chattel, mere commodities in a society where cows, sheep, and goats are deemed more important than women, girls, or mothers.

For most of us, the first human experience we have of unconditional love is with our mother. A friend of mine, who lost his mother when he was a young teen, believes that the love of a mother for her child, that unconditional love that the Greeks called *agapē* is, in fact, the first experience humankind has with grace. Mothers, and women in general, he argues, are special vessels of grace, both for their own children and for others. The disposition of the soul of a woman who is a mother is open to the flow of grace in a special way because of the powerful selflessness mothering engenders in creators for their creation.

I am not a mother. Not yet, at least. The deepest desire of my heart is to be a mother, if for no other reason than to experience that kind of grace. While I can't speak of motherhood firsthand, I do know a thing or two about being mothered—by my own biological mother and by many other people's mothers as well. When we returned with the Mamas to Millicent's house for lunch—a lavish spread of local delicacies prepared in honor of their visitors from Chicago—the Mamas mothered me in a way that forever changed the way I think about motherhood and grace.

As Maury and I traveled through Africa, we carried bottled water with us because potable water was hard to come by in some of the locations we visited, and even when drinking water was available, it wasn't safe for us to drink. For whatever reason, on the morning we visited Asembo Bay, we'd neglected to bring bottled water. Even our guides had forgotten to toss a couple of bottles in the back of the van, as was their habit. After several hours under the hot sun in the 90-degree temperature, I was parched. While we sat on an upholstered love seat the Mamas had dragged into the compound along with a motley collection of chairs arranged in a circle for our comfort while we ate, I started to swoon. In hindsight, I believe it was the first time I'd experienced true thirst with no way to slake it. The Mamas had well water, but nothing I could drink without the risk of becoming violently ill.

But I was a visitor and didn't want to complain or cause a scene. My mind swimming, I tried hard to concentrate on the presentation a few of the women did for us, explaining how nuns from a nearby convent had taught them about basic nutrition so they could raise healthy children, even given their meager resources. Some of the kids from Asembo Bay, dressed to the nines in frilly pastel dresses or crisp dress shirts, performed songs and recited poetry. It was a beautiful, terribly touching display. As I applauded one of the performances, two Mamas approached me from either side, worried expressions on their faces.

"She needs water," one said, summoning one of the older children.

"Take this," she said, handing the teenage girl a100-shilling note. "Go. Quickly!"

They didn't make a fuss. I could tell the Mamas didn't want to embarrass me. While we waited for the girl to return from the shop she'd run to a mile away, the women quietly brought me a damp cloth for my forehead and insisted I move to a chair in a narrow slice of shade. The presentations and performances continued, and lunch was served. Before Millicent offered a prayer over the food, another woman brought out a plastic bowl filled with water and knelt down in front of the first few seated women, who washed their hands and faces. She repeated the same ritual of kneeling and placing the bowl in front of each person in the circle. Dipping my hands into the cool, murky water and splashing some on my neck and face felt sacramental, life giving. I'd never recognized before how sacred the simple act of washing my hands could feel.

Soon the teenage girl returned with several bottles of cold (talk about miraculous!) water. When I took the first few sips, I felt as though I was a wilted plant growing turgid again as the water moved through my body. A simple, nurturing act of kindness — a sip of cool water on an unbearably hot day — brought me back to life.

After we finished eating, a dozen of the Mamas disappeared behind an outbuilding for a few minutes. They returned, led by Leonitta, singing and dancing around the circle. Holding a horsehair baton, Big Mama called my name and motioned for me to get up and join them. She is a fierce, regal woman with a broad smile and thick build and a sparkle in her intense eyes that I would imagine sparks fear in anyone who crosses her.

You don't say no to Big Mama.

So I danced awkwardly, doing my wonky version of the white woman's overbite, as the Mamas whooped and hollered, shaking rusty bottle caps strung on pieces of wire and singing in unison. They celebrated our presence, God's grace, and each other.

Before we left Asembo Bay, Millicent asked me to get up and say a few words to the women. As she translated my English into the Luo language, I thanked the women for their hospitality and joy and for the example they set for me of a kind of fierce grace I'd never before experienced. I told them how extraordinary their strength and ingenuity were and thanked them for taking care of the children and one another.

Then I asked if I could do anything for them.

My answer came in English from one of the youngest Mamas, a shy teenage mother wearing a red and black soccer jersey and a white kerchief on her head:

"Tell our story."

Perhaps what we are called to do may not seem like much,
but the butterfly is a small creature to affect galaxies thousands
of light-years away.

—Madeleine L'Engle

Annus Horribilis

17

A few years back, the Almighty and I had a bit of a tiff. We weren't so much talking, or at least when we did, it was in terse sentences through clenched teeth. Mine, not God's.

The trouble began when doctors diagnosed my mother with breast cancer. The news came as quite a shock for many reasons, not the least among them the fact that my mother is incredibly healthy, a flinty, seemingly indestructible Yankee straight out of the Katharine Hepburn handbook. That was the physical, personality-driven source of my shock. True to form, Mom handled the terrifying diagnosis like a champ, believing in the power of prayer and that God was walking closely with her through the good times and the bad. Her daughter, however, was having a harder time.

My mother is the most faithful person I know, a prayerful giant of unwavering faith. She's our very own Queen Esther in high-heeled espadrilles and a matching Vera Bradley purse. So, why cancer? Why her? I know you're not supposed to ask why, because there's no good answer. A very wise woman once told me that "why?" was a terrible question, that instead I should ask, "What am I learning?" It's sage advice, but still I wanted to know why.

The news about Mom came on the heels of another doctor telling us that my father might have Parkinson's disease. (His doctor's exact, oh-so-sensitive words were, "If I were a betting man, I'd say it's Parkinson's." I could have punched him in the face.) So there was that. And then ... Mom called a few days later to tell me that the date had been set for her double mastectomy and also that my godfather had died.

What in the world? On top of everything else, I was a god-orphan. My beloved godmother, who also was my mother's sister, had died a few years before, and as I understood it, the same kind of infection that took her from me also had claimed my godfather. As a result, by the time Thanksgiving 2006 rolled around, I wasn't feeling as sunny about the God of grace I'm always going on about. It's not that I believed God gives people cancer or smites them with incurable infections. That's not how this loving God I know works. I knew this.

But all the great theology and faith I'd fostered for twenty-five years or so didn't change the fact that I was really smarting. I started checking the sky for thunderbolts and being extra careful not to step in front of buses.

I felt like Job. And also like Marisa Tomei in *My Cousin Vinny*.

I had become a hostile witness, not unlike the scene in *My Cousin Vinny* where Tomei's boyfriend, Vinny (Joe Pesci), calls her to the stand as an expert witness in the murder case he's defending right after they've had a big fight. In the film, Vinny asks the judge for permission to treat his girlfriend as a hostile witness, and Tomei says, "You think I'm hostile now; wait until tonight."

In my scenario, God was Cousin Vinny, and I was Marisa Tomei.

When we first got the news about Mom's breast cancer, I sent an email to my closest friends asking them to pray for her and for our family. About twenty seconds after I hit the Send button on the computer keyboard, I received a reply from one of my best friends, Jen.

It read, simply, "Oh, f–."

About twenty seconds after that, while I was still laughing my head off, the phone rang. It was Jen calling to apologize, saying she hadn't meant that to be construed as a prayer.

I told her it was, in fact, a prayer. And a good one at that.

It's been said the two best prayers are "Help me, help me, help me" and "Thank you, thank you, thank you." And the great Christian apologist C. S. Lewis once said that what we think are our worst prayers might actually be, to God, our very best. In *Letters to Malcolm*, Lewis wrote, "Those, I mean, which are least supported by devotional feeling. . . . God sometimes seems to speak to us most intimately when he catches us, as it were, off our guard."

So, "oh, f–" it is.

It was a prayer. It was a start.

In the weeks that followed Mom's diagnosis, I watched the

petrifying unknown unfold as a date was set for her surgery, as she was wheeled away from us in the pre-op room to the surgical theater where she'd have both breasts removed, as we waited long hours in the family lounge for word of how she was doing, as I walked into the post-op room to see her lying there pale and fragile, with tubes coming out and an oxygen mask on, as I bent down to hear her first words as she emerged from the fog of general anesthesia: "Praise God." Those were her words, not mine. I was still trying to get there, hoping that sooner or later, I would.

A little friendly advice: There are two things a person who is in distress—hurting, mourning, feeling his or her worst—never wants to hear: "That which does not kill us makes us stronger," and "Everything happens for a reason." I heard both of them many times during my mother's cancer fight. And each time, I wanted to turn to the well-meaning, kind soul saying them by way of trying to console me and scream, "SHUT THE HELL UP AND LEAVE ME ALONE!" But I did not. I said, "I know," and "Thank you," and tried to keep my rage to myself. The funny thing, though, about rage is that you can't keep it to yourself any more than you can keep joy or the flu to yourself. It leaks out, contaminating the atmosphere around you.

Even as the news from Mom's doctors was all good—marvelously, miraculously great, actually—that nasty pall still lingered over me. While it turned out she had three kinds of breast cancer in one breast and one in the other, the double mastectomy got all of it. None of her lymph nodes were cancerous, and she didn't need to endure radiation or chemotherapy. Her breast reconstruction went very well, and she's enjoying her new boobs—she has cleavage for the first time—and accompanying new wardrobe. She didn't have any pain. Seriously. None. After her first week post-op, she didn't take a single Tylenol. A bottle of Percocet her doctor prescribed sat on her dresser, unopened. To look at her you wouldn't have known she'd undergone anything more taxing than a manicure.

So why with all of the goods news about Mom did I feel so thoroughly lousy?

Don't get me wrong. I was grateful, so grateful, to Mom's doctors, who quite literally saved her life; to friends and strangers, who wrote to us reminding us that their thoughts and prayers were with us and, more important, that God was walking by our side — carrying us when necessary — through dark times. It's just that I seemed to have come out of this ordeal with a pronounced limp, spiritually speaking. Having witnessed firsthand the power of faith and prayer to work miracles, I was limping along like a bear with a thorn in my paw. And I wasn't sure why.

Everything happens for a reason. Right? Maybe I'd be able to run marathons once my limp healed. Maybe. Or maybe I'd keep on limping.

Not long after Mom's surgery, a pastor friend of mine sent me a note addressing the whole limping, querulous, bearlike quality I seemed to have acquired. He reminded me of what the word "Eucharist" — "the good gift" — is all about.

"God's gift to us. Our gratitude. The Eucharist is where the body is broken and the blood spilled out," he said. "And so we're Eucharist for the world — we break ourselves open and pour ourselves out so that others may be fed. No wonder we're tired, deep-in-the-soul tired, sometimes. When someone has been fed, someone else had to have been broken and spilled. That's how it works. There have to be these times when we let what's been broken be put back together and what's been spilled to be poured back in. 'Cuz that's how we roll."

Roll. Limp. Same difference.

For some reason unknown to me at the time but known to my Maker, I was limping. I resigned myself to the fact that I might never know why. But I was sure of one thing: when whatever was ailing me finally healed, I'd be stronger.

As I am wont to do when I'm trying to figure out something big, I wrote about it in the newspaper. Putting my thoughts down and sharing them with others is cathartic and sometimes leads to the answers I seek. After I wrote about my mother's cancer, I received hundreds of emails from bighearted folks offering their best wishes, prayers, and advice. One note in particular, from a Chicago Fire Department paramedic named Tom Kalicky, was so touching I decided to seek him out.

Tom had sent his short note because he wanted to comfort and encourage me. I don't doubt this for a second. His motive was 100 percent altruistic. He didn't want anything from me. Instead, he wanted to give me something: Hope. Tom told me not to give up on my faith or on God.

"I just have to remember God loves me, cares for me, and wants what is best for me, even if I don't see it or have a clear picture of the big picture," Tom wrote.

And he should know because he really was a modern-day Job.

Sitting at their kitchen table a few days after Tom sent his note, I learned the Kalicky family's wrenching story. Tom's wife, Kim, a nurse by trade, was battling cancer and hadn't been able to work in almost a year. The fire department had just reinstated Tom on the job after he injured his back carrying a stretcher two years earlier.

The Kalickys' sixteen-year-old son was causing so much trouble at home that they had to send him to live with family in downstate Illinois, and then he was expelled from school.

The day Kim got out of the hospital a few months before I met the family, her eighty-eight-year-old grandfather called to say he'd lost his home and had nowhere to live, so they moved him into the basement apartment of their modest home in Chicago. Despite trying to work out a payment plan with their bank, the Kalickys were facing bankruptcy, and while Tom was working a twenty-four-hour shift, two men showed up at eight o'clock at night to repossess Kim's car — four days before Thanksgiving.

Kim, a remarkably plucky woman with the voice and spirit of a pixie and the heart of a lion, has lymphoma. She's been battling the disease since 2004. After surgery and many rounds of chemotherapy, doctors thought they'd gotten rid of the cancer. But it came back with a vengeance in January 2006. After a couple more rounds of high-dose chemotherapy, Kim had a stem-cell transplant, and by the time I met her, she was cancer free again. But doctors told her she still had only a fifty-fifty chance of survival.

And I thought *I* had problems.

"We've got hope," Kim told me, her eyes twinkling through long, thick eyelashes, the ones that had grown back, at long last, after chemotherapy had made them disappear. "And we've got joy. We've always got joy!"

When Kim's car was repossessed, the family took the money they would have used for a car payment and bought Christmas presents for the kids. An unexpected blessing. The Kalickys are born-again Christians. They laughed a lot, even as they recounted their tales of woe. "I feel closer to God than I ever have," said Tom, who married Kim in 1995 after they met in a hospital emergency room. He was a paramedic delivering a patient. She was the nurse on the receiving end. "I'm not cocky or arrogant," Tom said, by way of explaining the family's inexplicable joy. In the New Testament, "Saint Paul wrote that you should pray by being thankful for what you have and then ask for what you want, and you will receive a peace that goes beyond understanding. I believe I finally grasp that now. I can only hope the same for you."

When I learned that Kim planned to take the kids to McDonald's for Thanksgiving because Tom had to work a double and she didn't have the energy or the means to make a big holiday dinner, I offered to come over and cook for them. I brought most of the groceries. Kim taught me how to make turkey gravy and scalloped corn, and we bonded over our odd mutual affection for cranberry sauce out of the can. Standing in the Kalickys' kitchen, we all cheered when Kim finally managed to free the maroon-colored goop from its tin prison with a satisfying *shhhhlock*! It was a moment of pure joy — one of many.

After ten-year-old Taylor Kalicky said grace, we went around the table and each shared what we were thankful for. Sonny, the Kalickys' teenage daughter, said she was thankful that her mother was cancer free. Jacob, the youngest Kalicky, said he was thankful for "duncher" (that's what the kids called our dinner/lunch/supper meal) and also for God. Kim said she was thankful for her family, for the people in their lives who had been so loving and kind — the family had been especially buoyed by fellow members at their church who had brought a constant stream of meals and helped with transportation, money, and constant spiritual support.

Kim also said she was thankful for me. I didn't know where to put that. I'm comfortable with the idea that other people can be grace for me — it's probably one of the things I'm most grateful for, honestly. But the notion that I — with my moody faith — could be grace for someone else seemed far-fetched. But, I suppose, if Kim could be my grace, I could be hers. When my turn came, I said I was most grateful for my new friends and that I was thankful for grace. For being able to find it again, there, with them.

"That's what Pastor was talking about last week — grace," Sonny piped up. "He said that we'll never deserve it, ever. It's a gift that we'll never, ever, ever deserve."

Her mother interrupted, saying, "Yes, but we get it anyways."

"Pass the butter!" Jacob demanded in reply.

"Don't forget your cranberry sauce," Kim singsonged across the table.

And in unison, her children yelled, "No!"

In a more somber moment a few days before our Thanksgiving duncher, Kim told me that she has to believe all the pain and suffering she'd endured for five years was for a reason.

"There has to be someone who still has a lesson to learn through this," she said.

I raised my hand.

"I volunteer. Let it be me," I said. "I've learned my lesson."

Get me through December
So I can start again

—Alison Kraus; lyrics by
Gordie Sampson and Fred Lavery

Bear Repellant

18

Go outside.

Sometime today, walk out into the fresh air and just be for a few minutes.

Even if you're in the midst of the capricious it's-summer-it's-winter, it's-summer-it's-winter season that passes for spring in places like my hometown Chicago, and outside is perhaps not the most inviting place to be, just go. Outside. If only for a moment.

Look up. There, hopefully, you will find sky. Sky is good and natural and sometimes—even on a cloudy, grouchy day, even if you catch just a peek of it between skyscrapers or by craning your neck from the bathroom window that faces the alley — really quite beautiful.

Marveling at creation is easy to do when you're sitting on the porch of a cabin in the mountains of Montana, listening to the rush of a spring-swollen river and the occasional cry of two hawks that have been chasing a smaller bird around the hills all afternoon. I'm writing this in a place called Big Sky, and it is aptly named. They filmed the movie *A River Runs Through It* here, even though Norman Maclean, author of the book the film was based on, grew up fishing rivers about three hours northeast of Big Sky outside of Missoula. I can understand why they chose this location for the film, though, as here is perhaps the most beautiful place on earth, or at least as much of it as I've seen thus far. All of western Montana is like God boasting, "Look what I can do! Look what I can do!"

But you don't have to be in a place as preposterously pretty as Big Sky to reap the benefits of stepping outside. This is particularly true for those of us who have been holed up trying to wrestle something out — spiritually, emotionally, existentially. Take the example of Jesus. When he was trying to come to terms with himself — who he was in this world and who he wasn't, what he was called to do and how he was to do it — he went into the wild, whether it was the desert, the Sea of Galilee, or the garden of Gethsemane.

Outside, it feels like there is less standing between the Creator and us. There is a lingering visceral connection we can hear and see and smell, reminders of the bond between Creator and creation, like the mountain sage crushed up in the pocket of the sweatshirt I was wearing on a short, muddy hike the other day.

"In the woods, we return to reason and faith," Ralph Waldo

Emerson wrote in his 1836 essay "Nature." "There I feel that nothing can befall me in life, — no disgrace, no calamity, (leaving me my eyes,) which nature cannot repair."

The first time I stayed at the cabin in Big Sky a few winters back, I made sure to take with me the can of bear repellant — supplied alongside chocolate-covered huckleberries and sage-scented bath salts in a basket by the bed — as I went on a hike in the hills above the Gallatin River. In this part of the world, there is a very real possibility of running into a moose, mountain lion, or, God help you, a bear sow and her cubs on a stroll in the woods. I recall anxiously clutching on that first hike the bear repellant (which looked like a cross between an industrial-sized container of Mace and a can of room deodorizer), convinced that every crack and pop of a tree branch was a grizzly ready to eat my head. And if a bear didn't get me, I was worried that I might get lost and freeze to death like a human popsicle. I don't remember that first hike being terribly serene.

This time around, however, there was no bear repellant in the bedside basket. But the woods beckoned, so I put my vivid imagination and city-girl fears in check, pulled on some boots, and headed into the great outdoors.

In nature, whether it's Central Park, the Grand Canyon, a rock jetty in the sound, or a small patch of scrub grass with a sad, Charlie Brown-ish tree near where the smokers congregate outside our office building, we step outside what Emerson called "the splendid labyrinth" of our own perceptions so we can see reality more clearly. It doesn't matter how extravagant or seemingly meager our piece of nature is, it has transforming power.

A few days before holing up at the cabin in Big Sky, I had

attended a Passover Seder with friends in Bozeman, Montana (a thriving metropolis by comparison), where the rabbi explained to those gathered what the song we were about to sing, "Dayeinu," meant. In Hebrew, "Dayeinu" means, "it's enough." Passover commemorates God's mercy on the Israelites, as described in the biblical book of Exodus, when they were spared from the avenging spirit of God that killed every firstborn child in Egypt, where the Israelites were enslaved. God told Moses, his messenger, to tell the Israelites to put lamb's blood on the doorposts so the spirit of death, sent as a punishment on the Egyptian pharaoh who refused to free the Israelites, would pass over their homes. For once, the Israelites listened, and their children lived, while the Egyptian children — including the firstborn child of the pharaoh — perished. Not long after that, God delivered the Israelites out of slavery in Egypt, miraculously parting the Red Sea on their way out of town.

Pointing to the Bridgers mountain range in the distance, the rabbi said, "I'm a great believer that just plain being alive is the greatest miracle. When we look at that magnificent site from the window, at the Bridgers — can there be anything greater than that feeling? And so the Hebrew tradition is to sing 'Dayeinu.' Only seeing the Bridgers today — boy, that would be enough."

A Charlie Brown-ish scrub tree, or a tiny slice of sky, also could be enough to change everything.

On that hike/schlep up the side of the foothills above the Gallatin, I forced myself to climb higher to get out of earshot of the traffic on a mountain highway below. Winded, I was thinking about who I am — who I really am — and how odd it is that I feel as much myself standing in a pair of muddy Wellingtons in the middle of the Montana forest as I do perched in stiletto boots at the bar of Balthazar in New York City.

As I paused to catch my breath, pondering whether I am more urban goddess than earth muffin, one of those hawks came soaring toward me, screaming as it flew ten feet above my head. In that breathtaking moment, I felt as if my question was being answered, though I'm not sure whether it was a yes or a no.

Native American theology says that animals—hawks in particular—can appear as sacred messengers, carrying lessons to us from the Great Spirit. In their book *Medicine Cards*, Jamie Sams and David Carson say hawks "[teach] you to be observant, to look at your surroundings," and that hearing the cry of a hawk is a signal for the listener to pay close attention in order to discern the message.

God can and does use anything God chooses to get our attention. Who's to say the hawk wasn't sent as an agent of grace to catch my wandering attention and quiet what Buddhists might call my "monkey mind," which is more often than not swinging wildly from branch to branch on intellectual and emotional trees.

On the way back down the hiking trail after my encounter with the hawk in Big Sky, I stopped thinking and started looking and listening. That's when I realized winter was turning into spring before me.

Change was happening. Creation, and perhaps the Creator, was speaking.

I just needed to be outside to hear the voice.

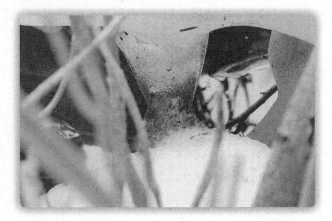

So we saunter toward the Holy Land, till one day the sun shall shine more brightly than ever he has done, shall perchance to shine into our minds and hearts, and light up our whole lives with a great awakening light, as warm and serene and golden as on a bankside in autumn.

—Henry David Thoreau

Cleopatra's Right Ear   19

First my mother. Then my cat.

I had no idea cats could get breast cancer until I felt a strange lump on Cleo's tummy and took her to see the veterinarian. It'd have to come off, he told me, and there was a good chance it was malignant.

Déjà vu to not quite a year before when an oncologist told Mom the same thing. The medical ritual for my cat was almost the same as it had been for my mother—first blood work, then exploratory surgery to see if there were more tumors, and if there were, more mammary tissue would have to come out. Then came the big wound with lots of sutures that needed to be monitored for infection, the bruising and pain, and a week's wait for the pathology report to come back, telling us how advanced the cancer was.

My personal ritual for dealing with Cleo's frightening diagnosis echoed my response to Mom's diagnosis. I cried, I worried, I got a little angry, and I prayed a lot. Just as I had when Mom got the news in the fall of 2006, I put up a post on my blog asking people to pray for Cleo. And just as they had with my mother, a lot of people said they would.

A friend saw my blog post about Cleo's surgery and asked a theological question I had not anticipated: "Are you allowed to pray for a cat?" My immediate response was, "Of course." God cares about all of God's creation, including kitties, I told him. But his question got me wondering what my own faith tradition and others really say about animals and prayer.

As I began to do a little research, one man's name came up repeatedly: the Rev. Andrew Linzey, an Anglican priest and professor of theology at Oxford University in England. Linzey, director of Oxford's Centre for Animal Ethics and author of a number of important books on the subject of theology, ethics, and animals, is the world's preeminent "animal theologian." Who knew there was such a thing?

"Praying for animals may appear a lost cause within Christianity, but in fact there are blessings for animals as far back as the *Rituale Romanum* of 1614," Linzey told me, referring to a text of Roman Catholic rituals, including blessings. "There is a great deal in the Bible that supports the compassionate treatment of animals." In the ninth chapter of the book of Genesis in the Hebrew Scriptures, God establishes a covenant with *all* living creatures — presumably domesticated cats included — and King David, in the biblical book of Psalms, writes, "The LORD is good to all; he has compassion on all he has made.... The eyes of all look to you, and you give them their food at the proper time. You open your hand and satisfy the desires of every living thing." Ergo, God's grace extends to all living things, not just us humans.

In the New Testament, in his Sermon on the Mount found in the gospel of Matthew, Jesus himself talks about God's care for animals. "Look at the birds of the air," Jesus says. "They do not sow or reap or store away in barns, and yet your heavenly Father feeds them." And Saint Paul, in chapter 8 of his letter to the Romans, alludes to animals being redeemed (along with humans) when he compares "the groans of creation to the pain of childbirth and creatures awaiting their redemption in Christ," Linzey reminded me, adding, "Redemption is clearly a cosmic thing and since animals are going to go to heaven, there can be no good reason why we shouldn't pray to God for them." Some scholars call that kind of theological take on God's relationship to all of creation "common grace" — as if something as superhuman and unfathomable as grace could possibly be considered common.

While there is no consensus among religions as to whether animals have souls and afterlives — most Christian, Jewish, and Muslim theologians say animals have souls but not the kind that live on after their bodies die, like humans do, while practitioners of Hinduism, Buddhism, and other Eastern traditions are more inclined to believe animals and humans belong to the same soul cycle of reincarnation — each has something to say about the care and kind treatment of animals. (One interesting bit of trivia I came across in my humble research was that Islam's Prophet Muhammad is said to have been especially fond of cats.)

There are plenty of examples of prayer for animals throughout the history of Christianity. Perhaps the best known comes from Saint Francis of Assisi, the patron saint of animals, whose October 4 feast day is marked in some liturgical traditions with an annual "blessing of the animals," where worshipers are invited to bring their pets and/or livestock to church for prayers of protection. If the lore is to be believed, Francis loved animals so much he referred to them as "brothers and sisters" and once even gave up his hermit's cave so a donkey could have shelter. Francis often is depicted with birds sitting on his shoulders, and one hand extended to feed (or bless) them. The carved, wooden folk art *santo* statue of Saint Francis that I keep in my living room has a bird on each of his shoulders and what is either a large spotted cat or small Holstein lying at his feet. One common Franciscan prayer for animals says, "Blessed are you, Lord God, maker of all living creatures. You called forth fish in the sea, birds in the air, and animals on the land. You inspired Saint Francis to call all of them his brothers and sisters. We ask you to bless this pet. By the power of your love, enable it to live according to your plan. May we always praise you for all your beauty in creation. Blessed are you, Lord our God, in all your creatures! Amen."

While I don't know that I'd go as far as saying I think of Cleo as my sister, she most certainly is a member of the family. Maury and I adopted her from the Anti-Cruelty Society about a month after the 9/11 terrorist attacks. We were so depleted—body, soul, and spirit—from the trauma of those horrific events that I think we both wanted something alive to care for, besides each other and the anemic Christmas cactus in the bathroom. Before we walked into the animal rescue center in downtown Chicago on a Sunday morning, we had agreed we'd try to find an adult cat, rather than a kitten, to bring home. Kittens are cute and are generally easier to adopt out, while grown-up cats have a harder time. We wanted to give a home to a cat that might not find one otherwise.

It took us about ten minutes to find Cleo. We played with a few kittens — I defy anyone (apart from the woefully allergic) to resist the powerful draw of a smushy-faced little kitty — and attempted to engage a number of adult fraidycats before we came upon a skinny four-year-old tiger cat with a gimpy right ear, black kohl markings ringing her big green eyes, and an upside-down white heart-shaped marking around her nose and whiskers. Her name, the tag on the cage said, was Cleopatra — Cleo for short. When Maury bent down and stuck his fingers through the cage, she came right up to him and licked his hand. We took her out of the cage, and although she was shaking and clearly terrified by the cacophony being made by a room full of people and other cats, instead of trying to flee, she clung to him.

An hour or so later, when we climbed into our car with Cleo in a new plastic carrying case, Maury gave me a speech about how we weren't going to become crazy cat people who referred to themselves as "Mommy and Daddy." Approximately five minutes later, when Cleo sneezed several times in a row — the Anti-Cruelty Society vet had told us we could take her home right away (rather than waiting the usual forty-eight hours) because there was some sort of feline respiratory infection going around the shelter — I believe the first thing out of both of our mouths was, "It's OK. Mommy and Daddy are here." A few days later, when Cleo's eyes had grown rheumy and she had stopped eating and drinking and was sneezing with increasing regularity, we ended up in the local animal hospital emergency room at midnight. "She's severely dehydrated," the vet said. "She has a head cold and when cats can't smell because they're stuffed up, they stop eating." He gave her an IV of fluids and sent her home with us, with instructions to watch her carefully, heat up wet cat food in the microwave so she could smell it better, and, if all else failed, shoot water into her mouth with a syringe. She might as well have been a newborn baby.

For a week, we fussed and hovered over Cleo, even moving a futon cushion onto the living room floor so we could sleep with her between us. The names Mommy and Daddy stuck, and our kitty, without us realizing it at the time, had helped us focus on something other than the horror of 9/11 and begin to heal.

When Cleo came home after her cancer surgery with a foot-long sutured incision where doctors had removed all of the mammary glands on the left side of her body, she was frail and traumatized. I lifted her onto our bed, and she let out a soul-shivering howl of pain. I lay down on the bed beside her, and she crawled up onto my chest and pressed her hot little face against mine, moaned, and fell asleep. It was as if she wanted to get as close to me as possible, like a frightened child. I stayed in bed with her for the better part of a week while she slowly came back to life. Cleo has such a sweet, gentle, and amazingly sentient spirit. In the seven years since she came home with us from the shelter, she has become a true companion, one of the greatest blessings in my life.

I remember the painful night my mother called from Connecticut to tell us that my Aunt Mary — my godmother and one of the most important, most influential people in my life — was dying and that we should get on the next plane home, I fell apart, wailing in a heap on the living room floor. Cleo came running down the hallway, meowing mournfully, and jumped into my lap, put her paws on my chest, and licked my face. She was trying to comfort me. It was remarkable.

Cleo and her younger sister, Mousie, whom we welcomed as a kitten in 2005, are a constant source of joy and delight for us. They're more like dogs than cats, sociable and affectionate. Mousie even plays fetch with balled-up pieces of newspaper. They are constant companions—by my side or at my feet as I work, and occasionally on my head as I sleep. I adore them and can't imagine life without them.

Nine months after her kitty mastectomy, I am thrilled to report that my cat, like my mother, is doing very well. Both, doctors believe, are now cancer free. And after successful radical surgeries, neither has had to endure radiation or chemotherapy.

The day Cleo had her kitty-mastectomy stitches removed, she was already pretty well back to her usual frisky self, so much so that in roughhousing with Mousie, she knocked over the statue of Saint Francis and broke his thumb.

Somehow, I don't think he'd mind.

Nothing a dollop of superglue and the power of prayer couldn't fix.

I come into the peace of wild things who do not tax their lives with forethought of grief.... For a time I rest in the grace of the world, and am free.

—Wendell Berry

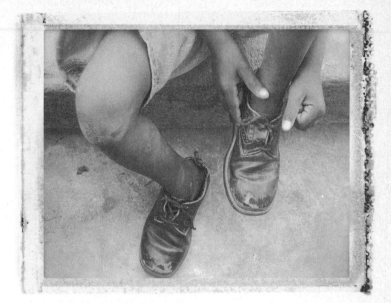

Chisomo

20

They warned me about this.

Along with stern cautions not to drink the water or eat any produce I couldn't peel first, not to take the anti-malaria medication that causes some people to have suicidal ideations, and never to leave my laptop or camera in the hotel room, they said not to get too close, not to let "it" get to me, not to become overwhelmed or "too emotional."

After three weeks of behaving myself and being cautious, keeping my head and heart in check while traveling through Africa, I did exactly what they said not to do. I fell in love.

Hopelessly, helplessly, achingly in love.

His name is Vasco. He's ten years old. It was love at first sight on my part, although I can't speak for the Malawian child who has broken my heart with his. As he sat on my lap and leaned his narrow back into my chest, I could feel his heart thumping — much too hard for a boy who was sitting still and hadn't been running around. Each beat of Vasco's heart shook his slight body so intensely that I could see a bulge on the left side of his narrow chest moving under the shirt he wore, the one with the word *chisomo* on it. At ten, he's the size of an average American six-year-old and weighs about half of what the suitcase I'd been lugging around Africa weighed.

I met Vasco in Blantyre, Malawi's second-largest city, when his caseworker, Mac, from a philanthropy that works with the city's many street children — most of whom are AIDS orphans who have nowhere to go or who have been forced onto the streets by family members to beg for money and food — took us to the outskirts of town to meet the little boy with the broken heart. At the time we didn't know what Vasco's medical diagnosis was, only that he had an enlarged heart with a hole in it. Basic health care for the very poor in Malawi is difficult to access at best, and treatment for specialized cases (such as pediatric cardiology) is nearly impossible to find, never mind afford.

Vasco pants when he walks, and he sweats in the shade. He doesn't complain and tries mightily to keep up with the rest of the boys. He loves soccer but has to settle for watching it from the sidelines. He smiles a shy smile, but I got the feeling it was more for my benefit than anything else. Orphans like Vasco get used to having their picture taken and smiling for strangers from a strange land who might be able to do something to lift them out of poverty and despair.

A few years ago, Vasco's mother and father died of AIDS, and just like an alarming number of children in this part of the world, he ended up living on the streets. That's where someone found him and took him to the philanthropy that works with street children, sheltering and feeding them until they are able to place the children with extended family. After months of searching, Mac located Vasco's aunt and uncle, and the boy went to live with them. They take loving care of him with their limited resources. When I visited the family, Vasco's Aunt Esme brought out a manila envelope from her tidy mud-and-wattle house and handed it to me. Inside was a wrinkled X-ray of the boy's chest showing an enormous dark shadow where his oversized heart is. One of Vasco's cousins showed me a plastic Baggie with his daily medication—chalky-white pills smaller than aspirin.

I only had a few days in Malawi and tried to do what I could to make sure Vasco saw a doctor immediately. But things move slowly in the developing world. And then there's the problem of apathy and corruption. When my husband and I told the director of the street children's philanthropy about our grave concerns for Vasco, he dismissed them with an emotionless "there are many children with many needs, and we can only do so much."

Mind you, this was after the director had taken us to a church service (at a fast-growing Pentecostal congregation where he's an elder) where, after four hours, the preacher hadn't preached yet, but the collection plate had been passed three times. When another elder announced that the budget for an upcoming celebration of the pastor's fiftieth birthday was $40,000 and asked the people to give more, I felt sick to my stomach, got up, and left. There hadn't been a word about the poor, the sick, or the orphans standing on the corner down the block. All we heard was the gospel of prosperity—a bless-me club for Christians consumed with the search for personal holiness.

As I leaped out of the director's fancy pickup truck at our motel a half-hour later, I basically begged him to make sure Vasco saw a doctor as soon as possible. He said, "I'll try to see what can be done." I wanted to slug him and then beat him with my Bible.

Vasco was the last child we met in Blantyre. Before we visited him at his aunt and uncle's home, we spent an afternoon with a number of other boys at a center in Limbe—the town next to Blantyre—run by the street children's philanthropy, which feeds the kids once a day, helps them with their schoolwork, and gives each of them a small plot of land in a communal garden where they can grow vegetables and homeopathic herbs to bring back to their families or sell at local markets. Two boys in their early teens, Steven and Elias, proudly showed us their plots with cabbage, peppers, greens, and artemisia—an herb used in traditional medicine that helps boost the immune systems of people who are HIV positive.

Maury and I sat on a stoop outside the drop-in center while two dozen boys ate their supper—a simple meal of stewed beans and cornmeal mush—in the afternoon sunshine. The boys were beautiful, so full of energy and playful joy. But there was pain there too. Some of their names hinted at the difficulties they faced from birth. One child was named Sizofuna, which means, we were told, "not something I wanted." Another was called Masauko, meaning "passion" (as in the passion of Christ). One shy boy's name was

Zalimba—"survivor." They were a charming, rambunctious, curious bunch who wanted to know about our life in the United States. Like children their age anywhere, I suppose, they were most interested in pop-culture icons. They asked me if I liked rap stars Akon, DMX, Jay-Z, and Snoop Dogg. Did I like Arnold Schwarzenegger, Jean-Claude Van Damme, or Jet Li movies? Not my cup of tea, but they're very popular with American boys their age, I told them. We did manage to find common ground when they asked about the actor Chris Tucker, whose *Rush Hour* movies with Jackie Chan they all had seen. I was a big hit when I told them that several years ago, I spent a few days traveling through the American Midwest with Tucker on a bus tour to raise awareness of the AIDS emergency in Africa among American evangelicals. One boy, a cutup named Vincent who had an unlit firecracker hanging from his mouth for much of the afternoon, could do a spot-on Tucker impersonation. It's amazing how movies have become their own universal language.

We talked to the boys about Barack Obama, the senator from Illinois who is running for president, and they were astonished that the son of an African man—Obama's father was a native of Kenya—possibly could become president of the United States. They wanted to know about the legacy of slavery in the United States and whether white Americans and black Americans get along. Maury talked about the kind of journalism he specializes in—investigations of wrongfully convicted men and women, including a number of people who were released from prison after his reporting showed that they were not guilty of the crime for which they'd been convicted—and I don't think he's ever had a more attentive audience. The boys wanted to know what jail was like in America and what happens to people when they're released from jail. In one heart-wrenching turn in the conversation, an especially bright, earnest boy said he thought he'd rather live in a jail in the United States than on the streets in Blantyre because the food would be better, because there are only two people to a cell where they each had a bed, and because in jail, they have television.

When the boys learned that I write about religion, several of them stood up to ask me the most peculiar questions: Do I believe in witches? Had I ever heard of witches who cast spells on children and steal their souls? What do I know about witch doctors and reversing curses? When I told them that I didn't think such things existed and that they were stories meant to scare them, the boys were absolutely indignant, insisting in loud voices that they'd seen witches for themselves and were certain what they'd heard was true. They told story after story about families they knew that had been attacked by witches in the middle of the night, and of children they knew who disappeared after they were cursed by witch doctors. Later in the day, Mac told us that such tall tales are common in the poorest communities and often are used as an excuse to justify turning children out on the streets—because they've been cursed or are possessed by evil spirits.

After supper with the boys, we stopped at another center run by the street children's philanthropy on the other side of Blantyre. There we met "Little Frankie," the only child who lives at the center full-time. Mac found Frankie living on the street several years ago and took him to the center. No one knows for sure how old he is or, for that matter, what his real name is. Their best guess is that Frankie is about eight years old. He was almost nonverbal when he first came to the center, and he didn't know his own name.

After a number of months, he decided to call himself Frank. It's a little clunky, but it fits, not unlike the oversized black wingtip shoes he was eager to show us he could tie himself. He's a darling little peanut of a guy with a sweet disposition, huge eyes, deep dimples in both cheeks, and big ol' ears that stick out like the actor Will Smith's ears do. With his short pants, floppy shoes, and mischievous twinkle in his eye, Frankie could be one of the Little Rascals. I was instantly besotted.

As he sat on Mac's lap on a wall outside the center, painstakingly writing his name with a pen in Maury's notebook, I asked Frankie what he remembered of his life before Mac found him on the street. In halting Chichewa, Malawi's national language, he said he didn't remember much except that his parents had died and that he came from "over there," and stuck out his arm to point down the road into the vague distance. Frankie's background remains a mystery. Despite several years of searching, Mac hasn't been able to locate any of the boy's relatives.

After our troubling morning at church on our last day in Blantyre, we stopped to see Vasco one last time on the way to the airport. Mac called his name, and we heard him yell, "I'm coming!" (in Chichewa) from the hut where he sleeps.

"Don't run!" Mac, my husband, and I shouted in chorus.

Vasco climbed into my lap, his rabbit heart thunk-thunking as he spoke softly, playing with my hands as I hugged his knobby knees. I told him I loved him and kissed his head. I wanted to throw him in my carry-on bag and run. (He would have fit.) But I couldn't do that. I had to leave him behind.

While I didn't heed the warnings not to get too attached, emotional, or involved, I did manage to keep a promise to myself

not to cry. At least not in front of anyone we visited. I managed
to keep it together until we boarded our flight from Malawi to
Tanzania, and then I bawled for several hours. I couldn't get Vasco's
face out of my mind. I desperately wanted to do something to help
him. Waves of rage washed over me as I realized the only reason
this child might be facing an early death is because he's a poor
African. If he were in the United States, he would be in the hospital
that very night, getting the medical attention he so obviously needs.

I've never felt so helpless in my life. It reminded me of a story
Bono once told me when I asked how he had become so passionate
about working to relieve the suffering and injustice caused by
disease and extreme poverty in Africa. Back in the mid-1980s,
when they were veritable newlyweds with no children yet of their
own, Bono and his wife, Ali, traveled to Ethiopia with the relief
group World Vision in the midst of a devastating famine. One
morning, a man showed up at their tent with his young son and
begged the young couple to take the boy with them when they
returned to Ireland. If his son went with them, he said, he would
live. If he stayed in Africa, the boy surely would die. As much as it
broke their hearts, Bono and Ali couldn't take the child with them.
"You had to say no," he told me. "Well, that's the last time I'm
saying no."

I thought about the Mamas in Asembo Bay, those fierce women
whose stubborn grace had made such an impression on me a few
weeks before we met Vasco. What would they tell me to do, because
I *had* to do something? I couldn't fix Vasco's heart myself, but I
could tell his story. When I got home to Chicago, I did just that,
writing about Vasco and his plight in a column for the *Sun-Times*.
The response from readers was astounding. People from all over

wrote and phoned in, offering to contribute to a fund for Vasco's medical needs. My friend from the Jewish Federation in Chicago sent me an email asking what she could do to help.

"Pray," I said.

"I'm not praying," she said. "I'm making phone calls."

My column ran on a Friday morning. By the end of the business day, she had convinced two hospitals to treat Vasco for free if we could get him to the United States. A family in the suburbs that had adopted a child from Africa offered to pay for his travel to the U.S. or wherever else he might need to go for treatment. An immigration lawyer came forward to help with bureaucratic red tape. Hundreds of people told me they were lifting Vasco in prayer, reminding his Maker to keep a special eye on the frail child in his little hut on the outskirts of one of the poorest cities in the world.

This is the point in the story where I'd hoped to say that Vasco came to Chicago, had heart surgery, and is on the road to recovery. But sometimes life isn't quite as neat as we'd like it to be. The process of having Vasco evaluated by doctors in Malawi so doctors here could determine the kind of treatment he might need, and whether he is a viable candidate for treatment, has taken months. Communication between the U.S. and Malawi is maddeningly slow. The good news is that one of Malawi's leading cardiologists has evaluated Vasco, and we now have a more specific diagnosis for the boy. He has a ventricular septal defect and an abnormal mitral valve and is suffering from heart failure. He's anemic but, blessedly, has tested negative for HIV. We've been able to help supply more nutritious food for Vasco to mitigate the anemia, and the boy has moved in temporarily with Mac in a more sanitary and comfortable apartment in Blantyre. He has a passport and permission from the

Malawi government to travel, and his immigration paperwork here is moving along.

But he's still in Malawi with his broken heart. And I'm still half a world away with mine, worrying and doing what I can to get him the help he needs.

Vasco is usually the first thing I think about when I wake up in the morning, and the last thing on my mind when I fall asleep at night. I cannot get out of my mind the image of him standing by the side of the road, smiling in his too-big T-shirt with a dove and the word *chisomo* on it.

His dark, sad doe eyes.

His delicate, almost regal features.

His whispery, shy voice.

That sweet, quiet spirit.

I rest, when I am able, in the knowledge that God is holding my darling African boy in the palm of God's hand, that it was no accident this child walked into my life, sat on my lap, and stole my heart.

By the way, in Chichewa, *chisomo* means "grace."

I went to Africa looking for chisomo. And boy, did I find it.

The heart is a very resilient little muscle.

—Woody Allen

Lagniappe

Most mornings here at the lake house the first thing I do after climbing out of bed is look at the water.

Then I put on the kettle, take the happy pill that helps keep occasional panic attacks at bay, wash my hands with patchouli-scented soap, and stare again for a while out the picture window at Lake Champlain, thirty feet below the desk where I write.

The first few mornings I awakened at the cottage here in upstate Vermont, the surface of the lake was so still it acted as a mirror reflecting moody clouds in the slate-blue sky and the foothills of the Adirondacks in the distance. Some mornings, even before I can hear the wind roaring through the stands of evergreens and aspens that flank the cottage, I can see it on the face of the water, churning the mirror into fussy whitecapped peaks.

I grew up along the coast in Connecticut, and no matter how bothered I might be about the state of my world or the condition of my soul, a body of water calms my spirit, the sound of waves lapping on the shore a lullaby. So when I saw the advertisement online for a "writer's bungaloo" overlooking Lake Champlain in a quiet corner of rural Vermont, it sounded like the ideal spot to wrestle out the final drafts of a book manuscript. The ad for the cottage promised "total isolation and privacy in what is truly the boondocks." No distractions. No TV. No neighbors to complain about the volume of the stereo or to catch me wearing flannel pajamas in the middle of the afternoon. "The only sounds are the waves, the crickets, and the intermittent aching moan of a train whistle across the lake," the ad said. Perfect, I thought. Just the water, the muses, and me.

When the tea is ready each morning—two sachets of Barry's Tea steep to a powerful brew in just under a minute—I put on my clogs and my old barn coat and take my cup outside for the fifteen-second walk to the bunkhouse next door where there is a working phone line and an Internet connection. As I hurry through the brisk and sometimes bitingly cold air just after sunrise, each day I have the same thought that comes in the form of a Bruce Cockburn lyric from his song "Wondering Where the Lions Are":

Sun's up, mm-hmm, looks OK
The world survives into another day
And I'm thinking about eternity . . .

I've come to think of it as my morning prayer. Good morning, God. Another beautiful day. I'm still here, and so is the sun. Thank you. Right, now let's get down to business.

These days the bunkhouse is empty but for the family of skittish gray mice that squat there when I'm not around and leave little chocolate sprinkles everywhere. But when I arrived at what the owner calls "Writer World" (à la the fictional Wally World from *National Lampoon's Vacation*) a few days after Halloween, I was not alone. I had unexpected neighbors: the eccentric owner and her faithful dog. I'll call them Julia and Brian.

Julia is an artist — a singer, painter, and performer — and Brian is a Shih Tzu/poodle mix, a stout, fluffy, white creature with a pronounced underbite and perpetual blank stare.

When I got off the plane in Burlington, Julia and Brian were waiting for me in the baggage claim area. She was wearing a fabulous tartan plaid cape and a black beret. He wore a sporty bandana around his neck. When, after a half-hour or so, it became obvious that only one of my two bags had made it to Vermont from Chicago, Julia and Brian set out to alert the authorities before I could figure out which way the complaint desk was. Normally, lost luggage is the kind of thing that makes me crazy, but I figured if my luggage had managed to make it through five separate flights from Zanzibar to Chicago the week before, it would eventually turn up in Burlington. Also, I had decided even before I left home for Vermont to assume a Zen position and roll with whatever this adventure in the north country had in store. Julia, however, was not quite as patient.

"Hey, are you anybody important?" she shouted at a member of the airline ground crew as I waited in a queue to report my lost bag. The fellow, wearing protective earphones around his neck and a huge walkie-talkie on his belt, smiled and shrugged. Brian sighed and continued to lick his hindquarters. I winced and made apologetic hand gestures toward the ground-crew guy and then at the busy desk clerks whom Julia had begun heckling. She thought they were ignoring me. I thought I might die of embarrassment. Nevertheless, in a few minutes I had described my missing suitcase, filled out the requisite paperwork, and received the happy news that the bag would be on the next flight to Burlington that evening and that a driver would deliver it to me at the cottage, an hour south of Burlington.

"He'll never find it," Julia shouted over my shoulder. "It's in the middle of NOWHERE!"

He'll find it, the clerk mouthed reassuringly. I smiled, thanked her, and followed Julia and Brian to the parking garage where their standard-issue vintage Vermont Volvo awaited. As Julia pulled out onto the highway heading south, she explained that she wouldn't be leaving the bunkhouse the next day as planned, that car trouble and some other business in town would mean she'd be sticking around for a few days. "But don't worry; I'll leave you alone!" she announced. She likes to announce things. It's the theatrical part of her nature.

I was a little surprised by her news, but, reminding myself of the fact that God has a fantastic sense of humor and loves to laugh at my "plans," I just went with it, chilltastic Zen writer/world traveler that I am.

It took Julia and me about five minutes to thoroughly cover our family and career histories before we plunged headfirst into religion. She was curious about what I do for a living — writing about spirituality and religion — and how I chose such an odd profession. I told her about attending Wheaton College and graduating from seminary, and about how I came to write my first book — a collection of conversations I had with famous people talking about faith.

"Do you go to church," Julia asked.

"I go to church for a living," I said, giving my stock answer.

"Do you belong to a church," she asked.

"Not really," I said.

So I revealed to her my checkered spiritual past. About first being Catholic, then Southern Baptist; about my stint as an evangelical mime in London when I was in high school; about the Jesus-loving Hippie commune where I used to worship; and about the last congregation I attended regularly — a left-leaning Episcopal church that exploded in a hurtful schism over issues having to do with homosexuality and scriptural authority, and about marrying my dyed-in-the-wool-Catholic-turned-freelance-Christian husband.

"Wait, go back to that Southern Baptist part," Julia said, interrupting, as she does. "Are you a born-again?" articulating her question as if she were asking me if I were really a headhunter or a Martian.

"Yes," I said, "but I'm not an asshole. At least not theologically speaking."

She laughed knowingly and asked me how I became, as she puts it, "a born-again." I launched into the unlikely tale of meeting my Maker while watching Jimmy Swaggart preach on late-night television. Like most people, myself included, Julia thought the Swaggart bit was hilarious. When I recount my spiritual life story—what the Southern Baptists called "giving my testimony"—the Swaggart part is always a no-way/way moment. It brings to mind something Frederick Buechner said in a documentary a couple of filmmakers made of him a few years back when asked what he made of TV preachers. Perhaps the best evidence for the existence of God (and Buechner makes a point of saying no one can prove or disprove God's existence) is that "belief in God continues in the face of the charlatans and phonies who peddle God on TV." It keeps me humble to remember that, in spite of Swaggart's perceived hypocrisy and public peccadilloes, God (with that holy sense of humor) chose to use him as a powerful agent of grace in my life.

"But you're still a born-again?" Julia said. "I mean, you were ten and now you're thirty-seven."

"Yep. I still am," I told her. "Once Jesus gets a toe in the door, he tends to stick around and make himself at home."

The term *born-again Christian*, Julia said, is a bad one because, even though she knows what it is *supposed* to mean, she thinks it's more of a code word for the kind of small-minded, mean-spirited judgmental Christians she sees on TV talking about divine retribution for the sins of supposedly secular society.

"You really should come up with another word for it," she said, as we turned onto a rural two-lane road and whizzed past the first of many dairy farms on the way to Writer World. "How about Jesusian?"

She has a point. Get back to Jesus and away from all the cliquishness of Clubhouse Christianity. "You could start a church here in town and call it the First Church of Jesusians (Reformed) and only let the nice ones in," she said. Julia was joking, but there was an important truth to what she was saying—this coming from a woman who doesn't have much use for organized religion but who is clearly and admittedly searching for something, for the kind of peace she hasn't found anywhere else. We became fast friends, bypassing chitchat about the superficial in favor of lowdown on the integral parts of our lives. That first night we shared a bottle of wine and more secrets. Then we watched *Harold and Maude* and talked about grace after the intrepid delivery guy from the airline showed up, as promised, in the pitch-dark with my lost bag.

In the days that followed, I settled into life at Writer World, figuring out how to work the cast-iron stove that heats the cottage, making a shopping run to the local organic food co-op, and learning the difference between one-year-old, two-year-old, and four-year-old Vermont cheddar. (There is no professional football or basketball in Vermont, so cheese appreciation is an important pastime. One deli owner told me that supposedly there exists a six-year-old cheddar produced locally, "but it's like a Yeti; I've never actually seen it myself.") Occasionally, Julia and Brian would appear at the front door of the cottage to yell announcements: "Get up, already, it's a beautiful morning!" or "The Internet isn't working!" "I opened a bottle of wine!" or "I have more of the four-year-old and crackers!"

I'd be lying if I said having Julia and Brian around was

just delightful. Frankly, I was worried that I wouldn't be able to relax and get down to the kind of soul work required in the writing process until I was all alone—as promised. But I made a conscious effort not to get all uptight and controlly about it. Still, their presence made me tense. One afternoon, I found myself in a particularly nasty mood when the new printer I'd bought specifically for the cottage refused to work. I plugged and unplugged it, replaced the printer cartridges, uninstalled and reinstalled the printer software on my laptop. Nothing doing. The printer just churned out blank pages. I tried not to think of it as symbolic.

It was one of those days where the lake was as flat as glass— perfect conditions for canoeing, Julia had told me a few days earlier. She keeps a canoe and two rowboats parked next to the fire pit on the shore below the main cottage. "I left the canoe out for you!" she told me. To the best of my memory, I'd never been in a canoe. Maybe once with my father when I was a little kid and we were visiting my grandmother in New Hampshire, but I wasn't even sure about that. I was, however, quite certain that I'd never piloted a canoe by myself. The notion of hopping in the canoe and paddling into the lake was intriguing, but I am, by nature, something of a chicken, and I figured the canoe would be nice to take pictures of for the folks back in Chicago—very Norman Rockwell—but that I wouldn't be taking it for a spin.

As I wrestled with the inert printer, cursing like a sailor, I heard something outside and looked out the picture window to see Julia and Brian in the canoe just off the shore. She was waving at me and shouting, "Yooooooooooooo-hooooooooo! YOOOOOOOOOO-HOOOOOOOO! Cathleeeeeeen! Come down here!" Julia is nothing if not persistent, so I abandoned the busted printer, threw on something other than pajamas, and headed down to the lake just as she and Brian slid the canoe onto the rocky shore.

Julia handed me the paddle.

"Should we bring a bottle of wine with us," I asked.

"Us? Oh, no, missy, this is something you need to do by yourself," Julia said.

"But . . . but . . . I've never paddled a canoe before," I protested.

"Get your ass in the boat and don't come back until it's dark!" she said, arms akimbo and eyes flashing like a crazy person. "NOW!"

"Yes, ma'am," I said, awkwardly climbing into the long silver canoe as Julia gave it a shove.

"Hold the paddle with your hand on top of the end, like this," she shouted. "Think Indian — like Pocahontas — in the mooooooooovieeeeeeees!"

Okeydoke. I paddled out nervously toward the middle of the lake, slowly getting the hang of it, each stroke stronger than the last. The sun was beginning to set, and there was a gentle breeze blowing. When I reached the middle, I stopped and just sat there listening.

I could hear the leaves rustling. A child laughing somewhere on the Vermont side of the lake. Some sort of a critter splashed up ahead — it was probably a water rat, but at the time I chose to believe it was a beaver. A loon cried its haunting cry in the distance. It felt like a scene from *On Golden Pond*.

As I sat there alone in the canoe, my thoughts drifted from Katharine Hepburn and Henry Fonda to Jesus and Saint Peter. In the fourteenth chapter of his gospel in the New Testament, Saint

Matthew tells the story of the time he and the other disciples were in a boat in choppy seas when they saw someone walking toward them *on* the water. As they often did, the disciples freaked out and shouted at the figure they thought was a ghost. It wasn't. It was Jesus, and he told the fellas not to be afraid. Saint Peter, who was bossy, yelled back to Jesus, "Lord, if it's you, tell me to come to you on the water."

"OK, then, come on," Jesus said, and Saint Peter got out of the boat and walked toward him on the water like a champ. But then he noticed the wind churning up the waves, started to panic, and then started to sink. Jesus put out his hand for Peter to grab, pulled him up out of the water and said, "O ye of little faith, why did you doubt?" Jesus and Saint Peter climbed into the boat, and the wind stopped howling.

It's always been one of my favorite stories from the Bible, mostly because I identify with Saint Peter, who has moments of great faith followed immediately by sheer panic. He always needed saving, especially when he didn't deserve it.

In her conveniently named book *Walking on Water: Reflections on Faith and Art*, that great spiritual giant and author Madeleine L'Engle reflects on the story of Jesus and Saint Peter walking on water. "When Jesus called Peter to come to him across the water, Peter, for one brief, glorious moment, remembered how, and strode with ease across the lake," L'Engle wrote. "This is how we are meant to be, and then we forget, and we sink. But if we cry out for help (as Peter did) we will be pulled out of the water, we won't drown. And if we listen, we will hear; and if we look, we will see."

The sun had dropped like the crystal orb in Times Square on New Year's Eve, and darkness quickly descended on the lake as I struggled to turn the canoe back toward the shore. Suddenly it was really dark. I was farther from the shore than I'd meant to be, and I wasn't sure where the cottage was any more. I started paddling toward where I thought it might be, visions of dragging the canoe on land and hiking back along the lake's edge in the pitch-blackness danced in my head. I tried to remain Zen, but was — O me of little faith — starting to freak out.

That's when I saw it — a flash of light on the shore about 300 yards ahead. I paddled harder, and the flash became a persistent glow. Then I heard it — Brian was barking, and Julia, who had lit a campfire, was yelling, "Yeah! Look at you! You're a natural!!" As I got closer to where Julia and Brian were waiting on the shore, I could see that she had gone up into the cottage and plugged in a string of fairy lights on the front porch. When I beached the canoe, she helped pull it in, gave me a hug, and handed me a glass of wine. Dinner — basil chicken sausage roasted in the campfire on a long stick, a brick of aged cheddar, and a pot of vegetable hummus — was waiting for me. We sat by the fire with Brian, sipping wine and talking until the chill of early winter caught up with us.

It's December now, and my work is almost finished. The Champlain has begun to freeze, ice forming like a zipper right along the border where Vermont meets New York in the middle of the lake. The fire pit is empty and dusted with snow. The canoe has been put up for the winter, high on a stone wall above the shore. And I am alone but for the chickadees and tufted titmouse that flirt from tree to tree outside the picture window, the year-round neurotic squirrels, and the mice in the bunkhouse next door.

In the weeks that have passed since Julia and Brian left for good, I have begun to realize that they were the muses I had been looking for here in the woods. I had neither planned for nor expected them, but they were the inspiration I sought and the kick in the pants I needed, even though I didn't recognize it at the time. Julia was a complete surprise, like Bernadette Peters in the Woody Allen film *Alice*, a classical muse (in full Greek regalia) who shows up out of the blue to help Mia Farrow (as Alice) with her writing.

"Who are you?" a startled Alice says when Bernadette appears late at night in her living room.

"I'm your muse!" Peters says, a little put out.

"My muse?" Alice says.

"Yeah," the unexpected visitor says. "You look surprised. I'm here to help you."

In her inestimable audacity, Julia was the catalyst in my life for something beautiful. I hadn't anticipated her — hadn't even wanted her, truthfully — but there she was. A little something extra that made all the difference in the world.

Plunge boldly into the thick of life.

—Johann Wolfgang von Goethe

Got to let go of the things that keep you tethered,
Take your place with grace and then be on your way.

—Bruce Cockburn

THANK YOU

Maury
  Joanna
    Mom, Daddy, and Mark
      Angela
        Chris
          Tracy
            Kelley and Bobby
              Kathy, Melinda, and Jason
                John Michael, Sara Beth, Anne Elise, and Lilly
            Jimma and June
          Elena
        Rob
          Bluestein
        Amanda
      Michael
  Rick
Dan, Christine, Mike, Britt, Aidan, Tim, Maura, and Casey
  Harold and Dorothy
    Nell and Jen
      Jessica
        Scott
          Curt
          Lyn
            Kelly H.
              Linda M.
                Carolyn
                Carrie
                  Linda H.
                    Allen and Ina

Mrs. Martin

Father John

Father Jim

Mrs. Sweeney

Annie L.

Frederick

B

Bruce

Irwin

Lin

Jean L.

Philip

Madeleine

Stan

Kevin

Marty

Laurel and Howard

The Kalicky Family

Aileen and Sheila

Ben and Mel

Pookie and Francis

Lori and Chris

Lisa and Shamus

Art, Nancy, Marcia, and Carol

The Sisters of Our Lady of Sorrows

Tall Guy

Tom, Tait, and Sarah

Simon and Sammy

Mac

The boys of Chisomo

Vasco

And . . . always . . . Linda Richardson

Credits and Permissions

The epigraph on page 8 by Frederick Buechner is from *Now and Then* (HarperOne, 1983).

The quote on page 10 by Louis Berkhof is from *Systematic Theology* (Eerdmans, 1979), 434.

The lyrics on pages 14–15 by U2 are from "Grace" (2000). Written by Clayton / Evans / Hewson / Mullen. Published by Blue Mountain Music Ltd. Lyrics reproduced by kind permission.

The epigraph on page 33 by Bruce Cockburn is from "One Day I Walk." Words by Bruce Cockburn. Copyright © 1970 by Golden Mountain Music Corp. (SOCAN). Used by permission.

The lyrics on page 35 by U2 are from "Walk On" (2000). Written by Clayton / Evans / Hewson / Mullen. Published by Blue Mountain Music Ltd. Lyrics reproduced by kind permission.

The epigraph on page 42 by Annie Dillard is from *Holy the Firm* (Harper, 1977).

The epigraph on page 50 by Thich Nhat Hanh is from *The Miracle of Mindfulness* (Beacon, 1976).

The recipe on pages 58–59 by Ric Orlando is from *We Want Clean Food!* (Clean Food Press, 2003). Used by permission.

The Bible quote on page 66 is from verses 5, 6, and 17 of Psalm 55.

The epigraph on page 75 by Leonard Cohen is from "Hallelujah" (1984).

The Bible quote on page 80 is from verse 5 of Nehemiah chapter 2.

The Bible quote on page 84 is from verses 3, 6, 7, and 8 of John chapter 3.

The epigraph on page 88 by Saint John of the Cross is from *Dark Night of the Soul* (1578).

The epigraph on page 95 by Joseph Brodsky is from the essay "To Please a Shadow," in *Less Than One* (Farrar, Straus, and Giroux, 1986).

The Bible quote on page 103 is from verse 35 of John chapter 13.

The quote on page 106 by Martin Luther is from *Luther's Works: Letters 1*, vol. 48 (Concordia, 1963), 281–82.

The epigraph on page 109 by Philip Yancey is from *What's So Amazing about Grace?* (Zondervan, 1997).

The quote on page 113 by Joseph Campbell is from *The Power of Myth* (Doubleday, 1988), 115.

The epigraph on page 116 by Rumi is from "Lord, the Air Smells Good Today" (13th century).

The epigraph on page 131 by Paul Simon is from "Graceland" (1986).

The photograph on page 133 is a courtesy photo provided by Sister Annunziata for use in the *Chicago Sun-Times* (2002).

The Bible quote on page 141 is from verses 34 and 35 of John chapter 13.

The epigraph on page 142 by Frederick Buechner is from *Secrets in the Dark* (HarperOne, 2007).

The epigraph on page 149 by W. H. Auden is from " Whitsunday in Kirchstetten" (1962).

The quote on page 153 by Seamus Heaney is from "A Found Poem," as cited in Cathleen Falsani's *The God Factor* (Farrar, Straus, and Giroux, 2006).

The "Dayeinu" litany on pages 157–58 is from *A Passover Haggadah: The New Union Haggadah*, ed. Herbert Bronstein (Central Conference of American Rabbis, 1982), 53.

The quote on page 161 by Maya Angelou is from "I Know Why the Caged Bird Sings," in *The Collected Autobiographies of Maya Angelou* (Modern Library, 2004), 49.

The epigraph on page 170 by Madeleine L'Engle is from *A Stone for a Pillow* (Shaw, 1986).

The quote on page 173 about the two best prayers is from Anne Lamott's *Traveling Mercies* (Random House, 1999), 82.

The quote on page 173 by C. S. Lewis is from *Letters to Malcolm* (Harcourt, Brace & World, 1963), 116.

The quote on page 175 about "Eucharist" is from Rob Bell.

The epigraph on page 180 by Gordie Sampson and Fred Lavery is from "Get Me Through December" (1999).

The quote on page 185 by Jamie Sams and David Carson is from *Medicine Cards* (Macmillan, 1999), 45.

The epigraph on page 186 by Henry David Thoreau is from "Walking" (1862).

The Bible quote on page 189 is from verses 9, 15, and 16 of Psalm 145.

The Bible quote on page 189 is from verse 26 of Matthew chapter 6.

The epigraph on page 194 by Wendell Berry is from "The Peace of Wild Things" (1968).

The epigraph on page 205 by Woody Allen is from the motion picture *Hannah and Her Sisters* (1986).

The lyrics on page 209 by Bruce Cockburn are from "Wondering Where the Lions Are." Words by Bruce Cockburn. Copyright © 1979 by Golden Mountain Music Corp. (SOCAN). Used by permission.

The Bible quote on page 216 is from verse 28 of Matthew chapter 14.

The quote on page 216 by Madeleine L'Engle is from *Walking on Water* (Shaw, 1980), 196.

The epigraph on page 218 by Johann Wolfgang von Goethe is from *Faust: A Tragedy* (1808).

The epigraph on page 224 by Bruce Cockburn is from "Mighty Trucks of Midnight" (1991). Used by permission.